Praise for Into th

"Lauren is someone who has fought the fight of faith. She doesn't offer surface platitudes or cliches. Hers is hard-fought wisdom. If you feel like you're going under, know this: God's hold on you is stronger than your hold on Him. As you work your way through the pages of this book, you'll be reminded again and again that God is good, His promises are true, and He will always make a way for you."
—**Susie Larson**, author, show host, national speaker

"*Into the Deep* is an invitation to a life with less fear and more faith, less insecurity and more holy confidence, less exhaustion and more embracing of all God has for us. This is a book Lauren has not just written but has lived with Jesus, and now she's offering us the same beautiful, life-changing opportunity."
—**Holley Gerth**, author of *You're Already Amazing* and *Fiercehearted*

"Lauren Gaskill invites us into the deep waters of courageous faith. Through the power of story and practical and spiritual steps, she reveals how to stay afloat when everything we know to do isn't holding us up. Lauren has lived this, and her words sit with us in the midst of our own battle, offering hope."
—**Suzanne Eller**, best-selling author, Bible teacher, and speaker

"I don't know a woman who wouldn't benefit from diving deeply into this book. If you've ever doubted God, struggled with anxiety, second-guessed yourself, or experienced frustration, this book is for you. Let me say it more clearly: *Into the Deep* is for all of us. Lauren Gaskill is a fresh, new voice sharing courageously and honestly about what it means to dive deeply into faith, even when the waves are tumultuous. I'm delighted to recommend this book."
—**Jennifer Dukes Lee**, author of *It's All Under Control* and *The Happiness Dare*

"Lauren Gaskill's *Into the Deep* is a biblically shaped life preserver for anyone who feels like they are flopping around in the scary, deep waters of life. She is a determined Jesus-girl who has seen God's transformative power through the 'deep' of difficult medical issues and the raging waves of anxiety and depression. Her book invites you to experience God's life-saving transformative power as well."
—**Barb Roose**, speaker, author, and life coach

"Lauren doesn't just tell us how to survive the deepest waters of life; she goes into the deep with us and shows us how to swim. Page by page she shares her heart of faith and inspires us to resist the lies of the enemy by focusing on the truth and foundation of our faith: Jesus. Lauren's personal stories and reflective questions compel us to evaluate our own faith in a personal and encouraging way."

—**Micah Maddox**, author of *Anchored In: Experience a Power-Full Life in a Problem-Filled World*

"In her conversational tone, Lauren shares how she has been in the abyss, questioning God and His purposes and plans, and how she has learned to dive deep with abandon into the current of life, safe in her Savior's arms. For anyone desiring to get off the safety of the shore and dive deeper into a more intimate daily experience with God, *Into the Deep* is for you."

—**Michelle Bengtson**, author of the award-winning *Hope Prevails: Insights From a Doctor's Personal Journey Through Depression*

"Lauren Gaskill has written a must-read for anyone who is no longer satisfied with the shallow end of faith. As someone who has personally walked the path of trusting God above all unknowns, she understands the fears and challenges that undoubtedly come with taking courageous steps into His will for your life. Her tender words will lead you by the hand as you learn to pursue God with reckless abandon. By helping to identify areas that hold you back and depositing truth that will propel you forward, this book will transform your relationship with God into one that is solid, steadfast, and undeniably rewarding."

—**Heather M. Dixon**, author of *Determined: Living Like Jesus in Every Moment*

Into the Deep

Diving into a Life of Courageous Faith

Lauren Gaskill

ABINGDON PRESS

Nashville

INTO THE DEEP
DIVING INTO A LIFE OF COURAGEOUS FAITH
Copyright © 2018 Lauren Gaskill

Library of Congress Cataloging-in-Publication Data has been requested.
ISBN 978-1-5018-6974-7

"Many Institutions Lost Ground in Last Decade" (chart) republished with permission of Gallup, Inc., from Jim Norman, "Americans' Confidence in Institutions Stays Low," June 13, 2016; permission conveyed through Copyright Clearance Center, Inc.

All Scripture quotations, unless otherwise indicated, are taken from the Holy Bible, New International Version®, NIV®. Copyright ©1973, 1978, 1984, 2011 by Biblica, Inc.™ Used by permission of Zondervan. All rights reserved worldwide. www.zondervan.com The "NIV" and "New International Version" are trademarks registered in the United States Patent and Trademark Office by Biblica, Inc.™

Scripture quotations marked (AMP) are taken from the Amplified® Bible (AMP), Copyright © 2015 by The Lockman Foundation. Used by permission. www.Lockman.org.

Scripture quotations noted CEB are taken from the Common English Bible, copyright 2011. Used by permission. All rights reserved.

Scripture quotations marked (ESV) are from the ESV Bible (The Holy Bible, English Standard Version®), copyright © 2001 by Crossway, a publishing ministry of Good News Publishers. Used by permission. All rights reserved.

Scripture quotations from The Authorized (King James) Version. Rights in the Authorized Version in the United Kingdom are vested in the Crown. Reproduced by permission of the Crown's patentee, Cambridge University Press.

Scripture quotations marked MSG are taken from THE MESSAGE, copyright © 1993, 1994, 1995, 1996, 2000, 2001, 2002 by Eugene H. Peterson. Used by permission of NavPress. All rights reserved. Represented by Tyndale House Publishers, Inc.

Scripture quotations noted NASB are taken from the New American Standard Bible® (NASB), Copyright © 1960, 1962, 1963, 1968, 1971, 1972, 1973, 1975, 1977, 1995 by The Lockman Foundation. Used by permission. www.Lockman.org.

Scripture quotations marked (NLT) are taken from the Holy Bible, New Living Translation, copyright ©1996, 2004, 2015 by Tyndale House Foundation. Used by permission of Tyndale House Publishers, Inc., Carol Stream, Illinois 60188. All rights reserved.

18 19 20 21 22 23 24 25 26 27 — 10 9 8 7 6 5 4 3 2 1
MANUFACTURED IN THE UNITED STATES OF AMERICA

To my sweet gramma Marlene Taska…
Your support and guidance over the years helped
me grow into the woman of faith I am today.
You are a constant comfort and inspiration. I love you.

And to my parents, Bruce and Jennifer Hardy…
I'll bring the tea, if you bring the cookies, Mama.
Of course, we know Dad will always bring the music.

Contents

Introduction

Take the Leap

"Jump! Jump!"

I stood at the edge of the pier, unsure of what my next move should be. Behind me, my sister- and mother-in-law continued their playful encouragement.

"Jump!" they exclaimed.

Part of me really wanted to. But one look at the seven-foot waves made me want to run back to the safety of the sandy shore.

The warm saltwater air beckoned me to dive into the cool blue ocean below, but fear arrested me to a motionless standstill as it taunted me with thoughts such as *You don't know what sharks might be out there; You can't even see the bottom; What if you land on something and hurt yourself?*

I closed my eyes and flashed back to the previous Christmas when our family had gone boating in the Bahamas. At one point during the tour, our guide invited everyone to jump into the open ocean. One by one, each family member cannonballed into the deep blue waters, but I stayed on the boat because I was afraid there might be sharks or I might get too cold.

Fear. From exciting adventures to everyday experiences, fear is a reality we all face. Our world is brimming with it. Headlines, social media statuses, and even some Sunday morning sermons are laced with twinges of it. We're afraid of nuclear warfare, unfair treatment, financial ruin, disease, and mass shootings. We're afraid God might not come through for us or even may have forgotten about us. We're afraid we don't have what it takes to make it through the tempests that rage around us. *Why are we so afraid?*

Standing on the edge of the wooden pier, I opened my eyes and saw that the waves were still crashing beneath my feet. But this time I decided that, despite my fear, it was worth taking the leap. Others had jumped before me, and I knew how to swim. I just had to have a little faith.

I breathed in the saltwater air slowly, letting it flood my senses and fill me with a calm, steady assurance. Sometimes we need to be reminded that the faith and peace we seek is within our midst if we would just breathe it in.

I asked my husband to count for me, and one, two, three, there I went, arms and legs stretched out wide into a star shape before plunging full force into the big ol' blue. The water felt cool and refreshing, and because I've been a swimmer for most of my life, I knew I didn't have to fear the waves. I knew how to stay afloat. I surfaced—a smile on my face and adrenaline in my veins.

A quiet laugh escaped through my lips, and I wondered why I'd been so afraid—why I'd let fear hold me back for so long.

I smiled again, knowing nothing was going to hold me back anymore.

This is what faith and freedom in Christ feel like.

Faith is not the absence of fear but the presence of courage. Faith says, "OK, fear, I know you're there. I see your big, mean, and intimidating self, but I'm not going to let you win. You're defeated in Jesus's name, and you cannot keep me from living the life I've been called to."

Beloved, you were not meant to live a life crippled by fear. You were made to experience deep faith, joy, and freedom in Christ. This is what our good, good Father so desperately wants for you. It's what God has spent the last ten years helping me find, and it's what I want to help you find too. I've learned that the way to find it is to dive into a life of courageous faith that helps us overcome every high and stormy gale as we commit to swim through life with Jesus. And that kind of faith is birthed in the deep waters of life—in the trials and the testings. This is where we have the opportunity to sink into despair or put our faith into action.

As we begin this journey together, there are a few things you need to know. First, the book is divided into two parts: Out of the Undertow and Swimming with Jesus. Think of each section as a progression in the faith journey. Before we can swim with Jesus and go deeper in our faith, we first have to break any chains that are binding us and keeping us trapped in the undertow. Then once we've learned to reach out in faith for the saving hand of Jesus, we are ready to become a true warrior of the deep: a strong, courageous, victorious conqueror and overcomer of the waves of this life.

Second, at the end of each chapter you will find questions for personal reflection or small-group study. You are free to write your answers in the book or in a separate journal—whatever works best for you. Finally, each chapter ends with a prayer prompt, which you can modify however the Spirit leads.

Beloved child of God, with faith and Jesus there is nothing you can't face and overcome. It's time to take the leap into the deep. It's time to dive headfirst into the unknown and embrace a courageous faith and relentless hope in the Lifeguard who is never off duty. This is where the real adventure begins.

We are more than conquerors through him who loved us. (Romans 8:37)

PART ONE

Out of the Undertow

CHAPTER ONE

Help Me, I'm Drowning

Deep calls to deep
in the roar of your waterfalls;
all your waves and breakers
have swept over me.

—Psalm 42:7

The clock digits rolled to 2:00 a.m., and I groaned, scolding myself as I tossed and turned in bed for the hundredth time.

You have nothing to worry about, and you're being ridiculous. Just calm down and go to sleep, I whispered to myself as I felt the waves of another anxiety attack creep up inside me. Sleep is a luxury for college students, and at this point I'd be lucky to have a few hours of rest. Every minute counted too, because I had a psychology exam at 8:00 a.m. But knowing this didn't stop my mind from racing, my throat from closing, my heart from palpitating, and my stomach from churning.

I clutched my comforter tightly and prayed for deliverance, but nothing changed. Instead I sank deeper into anxiety with each word I prayed. I wanted to jump out of my dorm room window and run until my lungs gave out. I wanted to scream until the anxiety drained out of my veins. I wanted to feel anything other than the sheer panic and helplessness overtaking my mind.

Minute after minute rolled by, and with no relief in sight I desperately reached for my phone and texted a friend from my Bible study group.

"Help! Please pray for me," I typed. "Feeling lost, alone, and overwhelmed amid another anxiety attack. I don't know what to do. I'm so afraid."

A few minutes later my phone lit up with a reply.

"My dearest Lauren, trust me when I say everything is going to be OK! God is with you, and He wants to use this for your good. Have faith! Trust Him and hold on to hope! He will see you through, and with His help you will overcome the waves. Always remember you are a daughter of the Most High King. You are priceless and beautiful in His eyes, and in Him you have nothing to fear."

As true as her text may have been, it didn't make me feel any better about myself or my situation. At this point in my life, I'd been struggling with anxiety attacks on and off for two years since my junior year of high school when I began having some health issues. To the outside world, I was an accomplished student and swimmer who had it all together, but on the inside I felt like I was drowning—lost in a sea of anxiety, depression, and unexplained chronic pain that was tearing my faith to shreds.

Week after week, I listened to pastors talk about a God who delivers us from our problems, but hearing their words only made me more frustrated and confused. I wondered: *If God loves me, then why isn't He rescuing me? If God is good, then why do I feel like I'm drowning in a sea of despair?*

Somehow I had missed the explanation of how a life with Christ doesn't always mean crystal clear waters or sunny blue skies; how God is not distant but swims with us through the deep waters of life; how God not only sends help in these situations—He is our help, despite what we might feel or think.

When my life didn't turn around and my health worsened, I began to doubt God's goodness. But worse than that, I lost faith in God's ability to save me. I tried to soothe the ache growing inside me by reading and studying the Bible, but none of it felt real. The stories seemed like a distant fairy tale—something only for people who had it all together and not for someone as messed up as me.

It was a slow process, but somewhere along the way anxiety and depression greatly diminished my faith. I stopped believing things would get better. I stopped believing God had a plan or cared about my future. I watched the world change and move on without me, and with each passing month the "water" in my lungs rose a little higher.

I was drowning.

By God's grace, after graduating from college I finally started looking for a Christian counselor. At the time, the cause of all my physical symptoms was still unknown. I didn't know that I had an overarching condition that caused chronic pain and put me at a predisposed risk to anxiety and depression. I didn't know that there were medications and natural remedies that could help me manage my health and start to heal spiritually. The only thing I knew was that I couldn't keep living the way I was living.

Within a few days of my counselor search, I found myself sitting in one of those infamous leather chairs. You know, the chairs all therapists have in the movies and on TV. The ones that make you feel comfortable and uncomfortable all at the same time. You're comfortable because the leather is super plush and buttery, but you're also uncomfortable because you realize you're about to pour your heart out to a complete stranger.

I grabbed a mint from the bowl on the table and took a long, deep breath as the counselor and I discussed how anxiety and depression were negatively impacting me. Our conversation felt like the very unraveling of me, but the outcome of it was a turning point in my life that helped me begin to understand how I might learn to overcome the waves pulling me under, threatening to take me out.

"Tell me, Lauren. What do you know about God?" the counselor asked as he sat back in his chair and clasped his hands, waiting for my reply.

Silence washed over the room, and I sat speechless, frozen in place. As I contemplated my answer, I hugged my knees into my chest and curled even further into the brown leather chair, trying to find the words to describe what I knew about God.

"I know He loves me," I began. "And He sent his Son to die for me."

"That's right...," he replied. "Anything else? Or, how about this question: What do you believe about God? I know you know Jesus died for you, but do you believe what the Bible says—that He truly loves you and fights for you, that He will never leave you nor forsake you, that He can make you strong and courageous, that you are no longer dead to sin but alive in Christ, that the same power that raised Jesus from the grave lives in you? Because if you can find a way to truly believe that... that kind of faith changes everything."

"Honestly? I don't know what to believe anymore. If God is good and worthy of my trust, why hasn't He saved me already?" I said finally, breaking into tears as the words left my lips. "All I know is that I feel like I am drowning, and most days I want to give up the fight. I'm scared, and I don't know what to do."

The counselor brought his hand up to cover his mouth as he glanced at the floor, contemplating the right words to say. And just when I felt like all hope was lost, he looked up and said, "Take courage, Lauren. God isn't causing the problems you are experiencing, but I believe that in His grace, He is using them to teach you something. Maybe this is your chance to reach out to Jesus and learn how to swim. Maybe it's time you embrace the waves and trade your despair for a faith that can help you overcome."

His solution did not make complete sense to me. After all, how does one go about trading doubt and despair for courage and faith? But despite my hesitation, I was willing to give the whole faith thing another try—anything to be rescued.

What Kind of Swimmer Are You?

When you're a competitive swimmer and your parents tell you it's time to apply for your first job, the logical, easy choice is to become a lifeguard or swim teacher, which is exactly what I did. Since my first lifeguarding job at Concord High School, I've had the pleasure of teaching children and adults how to swim on and off for more than eight years in four different states. Through this experience I've observed that there are three kinds of swimmers: swimmers who refuse to learn, swimmers who hesitantly learn, and swimmers who eagerly learn.

Three years into my teaching career, a couple in their sixties reached out to me for help in learning to swim. Up to that point I'd never taught anyone beyond the age of fifteen, but I was ready for the challenge.

"We figured since our granddaughter is learning how to swim, we should finally learn too, in case something happens and we need to help her or save ourselves," the wife told me. Though her face was riddled with hesitation in that moment, after the first lesson her reluctance gave way to an eagerness to learn. Four weeks later, she was floating and swimming in the deep end.

Her husband, however, refused to learn, and after the third lesson, I never saw him again. "I'll just stay out of the deep water," he told me. "I've been fine for sixty years, and I'll be fine for another thirty." I don't know if he will ever unintentionally find himself in deep water, but if he does, I fear what the outcome will be. Without the practice needed to build endurance and put skills into action, he won't stand a chance unless a lifeguard is present and paying attention.

Learning how to swim is a lot like learning how to exercise faith. We have to want to try. We have to pursue a solution. We have to commit to practice skills and work toward building endurance. Similarly, when it comes to exercising faith in the deep waters of life, there are three kinds of people: (1) people who refuse to exercise faith, (2) people who hesitantly exercise faith, and (3) people who eagerly exercise faith.

Can you see yourself in one of these groups today? I have fallen into all three categories at one point or another in my life. Let's consider each one briefly.

1. People Who Refuse to Exercise Faith

When my struggles began in high school, there were moments I refused to believe in the basic affirmations of the Christian faith. I rolled my eyes at Christians who told me to "just have faith." When I found myself drowning in despair, I picked up my Bible—not to read it but to throw it against the wall. I even stopped showing up for youth group and started isolating myself from my friends. When anxiety attacks kept me from sleeping, killing both my personality and my morning appetite, my mom lovingly tried to encourage me with prayer and a plate of peanut butter toast.

"I'm not hungry, and praying isn't going to change anything," I would tell her.

"Sweetheart, you need to eat," she'd say. "And you need to remember Jesus is with you. You don't have to be afraid of this."

I wouldn't say a word. I'd just take a bite of toast and think to myself: *Is He with me? Because I don't see Him doing anything here to save me. I'm drowning, and He doesn't even care.* What I didn't understand in those pre-college days was that I didn't see Him because I wasn't even looking for Him in the first place.

Instead of pursuing God, I obsessed over my problems. I didn't believe God was going to save me from the physical pain or anxiety I was experiencing, so I gave in to the waves of despair that swept over me, letting my arms go limp as I was sucked into the undertow. In these moments of swirling beneath the surface, the only thing I believed in was that I was destined to sink. So in a way, I guess you could say that I did have faith. But my faith wasn't in God; it was in my certainty of drowning.

If you're in a place where you believe that you're too far gone or that faith isn't worth the fight, hang on to this truth: the fact that you're reading this book is a sign that hope is still alive in you. Now ask yourself: *What would happen if I stopped refusing to have faith in God and started refusing to let myself drown? What if I embraced the waves, reached out to Jesus, and learned how to swim with Him? What if I traded my despair for a courageous faith that can help me thrive in the deep waters of life?* In this book we will explore together how to do just that.

2. People Who Hesitantly Exercise Faith

Sometimes we do not *refuse* to believe but we *hesitate* to believe. To hesitate is to pause, ponder, doubt, sit on the fence, think about, or seesaw and waffle (unfortunately, not the chocolate chip kind). This is where I found myself as I sat in that leather chair in the counselor's office.

Let me be clear: I should have drowned. When the waves became too powerful for me to face them alone, I gave up on faith. I can honestly say it's only by God's grace that I'm alive today. In fact, I believe one of the reasons He reached down and saved me was so I could share this message of hope with you.

The turning point came after hitting rock bottom in my college dorm room. In my weakest, most downcast state, I was afraid and hesitant, but I also allowed myself to ask the question: *What if?*

What if God could rescue me? What if I could learn to overcome the waves and swim in the deep with God? What if there was more to life than my pain and suffering? What if faith was everything Jesus professed it to be? What if the Bible's promises were true?

Asking these questions threw me into a big mental struggle, but here's what all of the wrestling taught me: Struggling is a good thing, because at the very least it means we are trying. It means we aren't giving in to the waves or refusing the possibility of a rescue. It means hope is alive within us. In the words of the band Tenth Avenue North, "Hallelujah, we are free to struggle. We're not struggling to be free."[1] God's love and Jesus's sacrifice have already set us free, providing a rescue for our weary souls. We just have to be willing to die to our doubt and cling to the faith and freedom we received when we first believed in Christ. This can be a struggle in and of itself, but holding on to faith and pushing back the doubt is worth it.

I wish I could tell you I am always eager to have faith. But after finally being diagnosed with Hypermobile Ehlers-Danlos Syndrome (hEDS) in 2015—which we now know to be the root of my chronic pain, anxiety, and depression—I'd be lying if I said I don't have days when I doubt or am hesitant to believe something. If that's you today, know that you're not alone and that feeling this way is completely normal and part of the journey! Just because we have hesitations doesn't mean we don't have faith. God doesn't love you any more or less if you're hesitant to trust Him one day and eager to trust Him the next.

The beauty of diving into faith, no matter how much or how little we have, is that when we reach out to Jesus, He is able to love us back to life. And in the flood of His great love, He longs to help us overcome any doubts we may have about who He is and what this life is all about.

As our Lifeguard who watches over and swims with us in the deep,

God gives us courage and helps us keep swimming when we feel like we can't take another stroke. We see this in Mark 9:22-24, when Jesus encounters an unbelieving man whose son is really struggling. Having no one else to turn to, the father asks Jesus to remedy the situation, even though his faith is lacking. "If You can do anything, take pity on us and help us!" Jesus said to him, "[You say to Me,] 'If You can?' All things are possible for the one who believes *and* trusts [in Me]!" Immediately the father of the boy cried out [with a desperate, piercing cry], saying, "I do believe; help [me overcome] my unbelief" (AMP).

Beloved, if your faith is being weakened by doubts and hesitations, God can help you overcome the unbelief you're grappling with. I'm living proof that all we have to do is have the courage to ask God to give us the faith we need to keep seeking Him—for when we seek, we will find the Savior we are looking for (Jeremiah 29:13). It's not an immediate, Band-Aid-type solution, but it's a permanent promise; and if we will lean in to God's process and trust in His timing, we will see great beauty and transformation unfold in our lives as a result of our faith.

We don't need to have all the answers; we just need to have a heart that is willing to reach out for the Lifeguard who can rescue us and teach us to swim in deep waters.

3. People Who Eagerly Exercise Faith

I never thought God would restore my faith and make me an eager believer—someone who courageously embraces the waves and overcomes because of the faith she has found in Christ. But my testimony gives evidence that it can happen to anyone who willingly seeks God.

As I hinted earlier, I've had my fair share of doubtful days, but over time as I asked God to increase my desire for Him, He replaced my hesitancy with an eagerness to pursue and trust Him more. With this desire also came a hunger for God's Word. For the first time in my life, I *craved* quiet time and joyfully declared Bible verses over my circumstances. And you know what happened? Yes, the waves were still raging around me, but suddenly I wasn't drowning! It's hard for me to put the experience into words, but when I finally put all my faith in Jesus, saving hope entered my story. The darkness beneath my feet suddenly did not seem so dark, and if I squinted, I could see a tiny light shining through my despair.

Every verse I declared over my life brought new light and hope, and in the dawning of the light my prayers shifted. Instead of praying with desperation or hesitation, I began to pray with boldness.

Lord, thank You for never giving up on me. Thank You for allowing me to fall into the deep, where waves can encourage a deeper faith in You. I'll never understand Your love for me or why You saved me from drowning, but for the first time in my life, I believe that You are with me. I believe that You want to help me and will use this for my good. I believe that You will not let me drown and that You will always rescue me. Jesus, I trust You! And I can't believe I'm saying this, but I think I'm finally ready to embrace these waves with You. Take me deeper into You, Jesus. Increase my faith. Make me strong. Because the deeper I dive into relationship with You, the more courageous I become. This is what I know: With You, I will overcome. Keep holding on to me, Lord. In Jesus's name. Amen.

Prayers like this became my saving grace.

I used to be apathetic about going deeper in my relationship with God. The truth is, when life was all rainbows, butterflies, unicorns, and cupcakes, I was perfectly content practicing a superficial faith and hanging out in the shallows.

Life is easier when it only requires a shallow-end faith. We don't have to learn how to swim because we can feel and see our feet planted firmly on the ground. We don't have to rely on Jesus and His Word to carry us through the waves because they are smaller in the shallows—barely a ripple. We can just hang out in a doughnut floaty while we sip iced lattes and soak up the sun, completely undisturbed.

But someday, whether by choice or by force, the wind will pick up and sweep us off our feet into deeper waters where the waves have the potential to take us out. Jesus promises us in John 16:33 (NLT), "Here on earth you will have many trials and sorrows." But God's Word also tells us He's not going to let us drown in those trials, because He will never fail or abandon us (Deuteronomy 31:6 NLT).

When we reach this threshold in life—the breaking point between the shallow end and uncharted, deeper waters—we have two options. We can sink deep into despair, or we can answer God's invitation to dive into faith, where we learn to rely on Him to help us overcome the waves.

The Choice We All Have to Make

You know how you can acknowledge something as truth your entire life but never really believe it for yourself? That was me when it came to pursuing God, exercising faith, and believing in the power and validity of God's Word. I was raised in the church and memorized my share of Bible verses. I knew Jesus loved me and died for my sins. And yet as a young adult, the reality of what it meant for my life never hit home. When I looked at the world, God's truth seemed true for the lucky ones and a pipe dream for the rest of us. I never really understood that Jesus didn't "come to call the righteous, but sinners" (Mark 2:17).

I touched on this earlier, but I want to say it again: There is a difference between knowing and believing God, and believing changes everything. But we have to want to believe; we have to want to be rescued. Which begs the question, do you want to be rescued? Do you want to go beyond simply knowing God to trusting Him with every fiber of your being? Do you want to exchange double-minded thoughts for a faithful, steadfast mind?

In John 5 we meet a man who, despite his hopelessness, desperately wanted to be rescued. After living as a paralytic for thirty-eight years, he had no hope of being healed. But that was before he met Jesus.

> When Jesus saw him lying there and learned that he had been in this condition for a long time, he asked him, "Do you want to get well?"
>
> "Sir," the invalid replied, "I have no one to help me into the pool when the water is stirred. While I am trying to get in, someone else goes down ahead of me."
>
> Then Jesus said to him, "Get up! Pick up your mat and walk." At once the man was cured; he picked up his mat and walked."
>
> (John 5:6-9)

What's interesting about this story is that the man didn't even know who Jesus was when He healed him. It's not until verse 14 that we read he learned who Jesus was and went to tell the Jewish leaders about the miraculous healing. Because of this, we know the man was healed not because of his knowledge of Jesus but because of his faith in Jesus. The Savior told him to pick up his mat and walk, and that's exactly what he did. He could have sat there and complained more about his situation or told Jesus that he was crazy, but he didn't. He believed Jesus's word over his life and put faith into action by following His instructions. So while the man's first steps of faith may have been small, God honored them and rescued him from the hopelessness of his situation. When we put our faith in Jesus, He is faithful to do the same for us.

Shortly after my initial appointment with the counselor, I took the first step of faith I'd taken in a long time. I asked God to help me see and believe the Bible for what it truly is—much more than words on a page.

As Hebrews 4:12 (NLT) puts it, "The Word of God is alive and powerful. It is sharper than the sharpest two-edged sword, cutting between soul and spirit, between joint and marrow."

As I worked my way through the New Testament, I began highlighting some of my favorite "faith verses"; and when I came to Romans 10:17 (NASB), the words stopped me dead in my tracks: "So faith comes from hearing, and hearing by the word of Christ."

The conviction I felt after reading this verse was palpable, and in my soul I knew why I had been stuck in the undertow of despair for so long: somewhere along the way I had stopped reading and believing God's Word for my life—practices that are necessary to grow in faith. I had settled for a faux, shallow-end faith for the bulk of my childhood, which served me well until the wind and waves swept me off my feet and I discovered that I didn't know how to exercise faith. I can only imagine how things might have been different for me if I'd chosen to go deeper in my relationship with God *before* the waves came rushing in.

The waters that you think might drown you are the same waters Jesus wants to use to deepen your faith.

We all need a faith that goes beyond knowledge to belief—a faith that trusts in Jesus to rescue us from sinking when we find ourselves in over our heads.

Maybe you can relate to my story. Perhaps you grew up in a Christian home and were taught that Jesus loves you, but you find that difficult to believe now because the world has beaten you down. You've been swept off your feet against your will and don't know what to do. God's Word seems distant, cold, or useless. Or perhaps you weren't taught that Jesus loves you, and you're struggling to make sense of the world. The water is rising over your head, and you're skeptical or afraid of giving this whole faith thing a try. You're afraid of what might happen or what God might ask you to do if you reach out and trust Him.

Wherever you find yourself today, I pray you will hear me when I say that the only way to survive and thrive in this life is to develop a faith that can survive the deep and all of its troubles and uncertainties. And you don't have to be afraid, because you are not alone in this journey. Jesus is with you, and He wants to be your Lifeguard and swim teacher. I'm also here as a friend to swim beside you as we navigate these waters together.

There is saving power in the deep, my friend. And the waters that you think might drown you are the same waters Jesus wants to use to deepen your faith.

Joy is not the absence of problems but rather the presence of a Savior.

This book is a guide for the journey, one that includes my story and the stories of others who struggled in the deep before reaching out for Jesus. It is an invitation to dive headfirst into faith, leaving fear behind in exchange for the boldness and courage that come from relying on Christ. My prayer is that through its pages you will learn to swim with God as deep calls to deep (Psalm 42:7), where joy is not the absence of problems but rather the presence of a Savior.

The world may seem like a hopeless place, but hope is right in front of us—right in our midst—if we would just have the eyes to seek and find it.

Beloved, it's time to stop entertaining thoughts of sinking and learn to swim.

GOING DEEPER

1. What do you believe about God? Take out a sheet of paper and write down everything that comes to mind.

2. What has been or is currently the biggest hurdle in your faith journey?
3. Have you ever struggled or are you currently struggling with doubt or unbelief? After reading this chapter, what is God saying to you?
4. What is holding you back from diving deeper into faith today?

PRAYER

Father God, Thank You for being a God who loves deeply. Your love is overwhelming, all-consuming, reckless, and wonderful. Thank You for never giving up on me. I confess I haven't always been serious about my faith, and I am still unsure about so many things, but Father, I need You. I believe You sent Your Son to die on a cross for my sins. I believe Jesus rose again and conquered sin and death so I could be free in You. Lord, help my unbelief. Increase my faith today. I want You to be the air I breathe, the song I sing, the reason I live, and the One who helps me keep swimming no matter what. Be my everything, Jesus. In Your holy, precious name. Amen.

When to Seek Professional Help

Everyone feels down in the dumps, stressed, or anxious from time to time, but if your depressed or anxious mood lasts for more than two weeks and is affecting your quality of life (relationships, career, thought life), it might be a good idea to consult a mental health professional. If you are contemplating suicide, you should seek immediate help. Do not pass GO. Do not collect $200. Seek help. It might just save your life.

Something to keep in mind: Traditional medicine works for some but can actually maximize symptoms for others. I have friends who swear by antidepressants and do well with them. In my own experience a particular medication put me in danger. The best thing you can do is talk to your doctor about treatment options and keep an open, positive mind while you try to figure out what works best for *you*.

Today I take a combination of natural remedies to keep my symptoms at bay. The best advice I can offer on this matter is to be patient as you work with your medical and/or mental health professional and pray for the Lord to guide you down the treatment path He wants you to take. Whatever remedy God provides, know that anxiety and depression don't make you any less of a Christian. And God gives us doctors and medicine to help us when we can't help ourselves.

CHAPTER TWO

Where Is Our Faith?

I know now, Lord, why you utter no answer.
You are yourself the answer.
Before your face questions die away.
What other answer would suffice?

—C. S. Lewis[1]

A smile crept across my face as I walked down the amphitheater rows to find my seat. With downtown Raleigh behind me, the smell of soft pretzels in the air all around me, and only six minutes to spare until one of my favorite bands took the spotlight, it was a blissful summer night. The kind that makes you feel free. The kind that makes your soul come alive.

My husband, Alex, had surprised me on my birthday with tickets to see the Goo Goo Dolls, a band we listened to when we first started dating in high school. But while I had expected the night to be full of nostalgia and celebration, my experience turned out to be quite different.

I knew that the band had been starting their set list with a song called "Over and Over," so I settled into my seat, ready to hear the song I thought was coming. But as the band began to play and sing, the opener turned out to be quite different from what I'd expected. What I didn't know was that midyear the band had debuted a new single, "Tattered Edge / You Should Be Happy," as their opener.

I wanted to like the new song, but the lyrics broke my heart with each word I heard. I looked around the venue as they sang about the tattered condition of our world, our nation, and even our own lives; and what I saw ripped me in two. I saw men and women shouting along in anger and desperation. I saw people rolling their eyes. I saw people shaking their heads as they stood with their eyes closed, heads bowed toward the ground. I saw people staring into space—not a trace of emotion on their faces.

"Oh, all we need is something real to believe in."[2]

Over and over again, the band sang these words, and all I could do in response was say to myself and Alex, "That something they are singing about . . . that something everyone is missing . . . it's faith in God!"

The answer to our brokenness and distress isn't an earthly solution; it's a heavenly one.

Sure, the world is messed up and broken. We're all broken. That's part of the human condition. But in our search for something to believe in, what the world is missing is *real* hope. And that hope—that something to believe in—is Jesus Christ.

Politics can't save us. Songs can't rescue us. Designer jeans and other material things can't pull us out of the undercurrents of despair. They can numb the pain for a little bit, but they will never fix our situation. The answer to our brokenness and distress isn't an earthly solution; it's a heavenly one.

The world can't give us something "real" to believe in. The answer we're looking for cannot be found in a superstar, spouse, child, friend, church, pastor, nation, lifestyle, job, bank account, or healthy body. Only God gives us something real to believe in, and it's the power of *true* faith—an unshakable trust in the One True God who is Creator, Sustainer, and Father of the Son who endured death on a cross to rise again and redeem those who choose to follow Him. What other religious figure or object can claim this feat? None but Jesus. He is the answer we've been looking for all along.

So before we can continue on this journey, first we have to ask ourselves: *What's the object of our faith today?*

Faith Lost

I could hear them talking through the cubicle wall about something from the morning news, and the angst laced within their words made me cringe.

"I don't know what to believe in anymore. What's wrong with this country?" the first person said.

Another voice shouted, "This country is completely going down the drain. If anybody in this office disagrees with me, we are no longer friends."

I'm not sure what my coworkers hoped their assertions would accomplish, but their passionate outbursts are representative of the divided state of our nation on so many different issues. The press has called us the "Divided States of America"—or, as many news reports put it, a faithless nation that has given up hope on its government and on each other.[3] All you have to do is hop on social media to see the division—even among believers. The very people who proclaim faith in Jesus Christ—who preach love and unity—often are arguing and bickering with one another just like everyone else. The maddening commentaries have left many feeling disgusted and hopeless, and we can't help wondering how we've become so faithless in each other and in our great God.

While the rise of faithlessness may seem sudden to some, researchers have been collecting data around this social trend for decades, and their findings support a growing epidemic of unbelief and general distrust in our nation. According to a Gallup poll, trust in our political, educational, social, and religious institutions has slid to a historic low, with just 32 percent of people expressing faith and confidence in the systems that run this nation. Specifically, television news, newspapers, Congress, banks, and church or organized religion are some of the categories where the most trust has been lost (see the Difference column in the chart below).[4]

Many Institutions Lost Ground in Last Decade

Percentage with "a great deal" or "quite a lot" of confidence in the institution

	June 2006	June 2016	Difference, 2006 to 2016
	%	%	pct. pts.
Military	73	73	0
Police	58	56	-2
Church or organized religion	52	41	-11
Medical system	38	39	+1
Presidency	33	36	+3
U.S. Supreme Court	40	36	-4
Public schools	37	30	-7
Banks	49	27	-22
Organized labor	24	23	-1
Criminal justice system	25	23	-2
Television news	31	21	-10
Newspapers	30	20	-10
Big business	18	18	0
Congress	19	9	-10

GALLUP POLLS, JUNE 1-4, 2006, AND JUNE 1-5, 2016

These data points suggest that the majority of people in our country disapprove of the institutions that are meant to help them and make their lives better, including the church. More than ever before, people don't know what to believe in. They don't know whom to trust. Laura Hansen, at Western New England University, observed:

We have lost our gods....We lost [faith] in the media: Remember Walter Cronkite? We lost it in our culture: You can't point to a movie star who might inspire us, because we know too much about them. We lost it in politics, because we know too much about politicians' lives. We've lost it—that basic sense of trust and confidence—in everything.[5]

It's not just Americans who have lost faith. Faithlessness has become a global epidemic. Israel, Britain, Australia—these are just some of the other nations mirroring the global trend of dissatisfaction and cynicism.[6] In a world that has lost faith in the things we can see, it's no wonder we've also lost faith in the things we cannot see.

Belief in God has been dwindling for years in many places in the world, but it has reached an all-time low in our nation, with a whopping 23 percent of the population declaring themselves unaffiliated with any religion, according to a Pew Research Study.[7] Though as Christians we know who we can and should trust, how often are we swept into heated conversations that cause us to inadvertently doubt or question the truth about some point of our faith?

A couple of years ago the *New York Times* aired a commercial that created a lot of buzz around the marketing agency I worked for at the time. Though I didn't catch it live, I watched it online. At first glance the TV spot didn't look like much. There were no special effects or people on screen— just a simple, monochromatic color scheme and a series of words. But three seconds into the spot, a series of sentences began to flash and fade across the screen. Meanwhile a barrage of voices shouted headlines and claims in the background, making it hard to understand what was being communicated. Even though the words were right in front of my face, I couldn't focus on the message. I didn't know what or who to listen to; I just wanted the noise to stop.

When the commercial ended, I watched it muted a second time to get a better understanding of the message. The last three sentences stuck with me: "The truth is hard to find. The truth is hard to know. The truth is more important now than ever."[8]

They are right about one thing: the truth is more important now than ever. But they're wrong about truth being hard to find and know. It's right in front of us, and it's worth putting our faith in because it's better than anything this world could ever offer.

Faith Restored

As a young teenager, one of my favorite recording artists was Natalie Grant. I'd put her CD in my Walkman, press play, and dance around our backyard as if I were the one performing on stage in front of thousands of people. I didn't want to be Natalie Grant, but I fiercely looked up to her, among other superstars. In my mind, singers, movie stars, news anchors, and anyone in the spotlight were untouchable. They seemed to live their lives on a different level—what I thought of as an almost angelic level that only special people reached. My life was full of imperfections, but their lives seemed to be a flawless dream that made me want to trade places with them.

You can imagine my confusion one afternoon when my mom started talking about how a beloved Christian singer was battling cancer.

"But superstars don't get sick," I told her confidently.

She chuckled and ruffled my hair, saying, "Sweetie, people in the spotlight are no different from you and me. They get sick and face difficulties just like the rest of us. They aren't perfect, and they make mistakes too."

Being the trusting soul that I was, I didn't question my mom. What I did begin to question, however, was how I could put my hope and confidence in other people. I may have been young in my faith, but it didn't take long for me to see that I had been placing my faith in the wrong things.

Somewhere along the way I'd put the superstars of my day on a higher level than God, elevating their lives above everything else and letting their opinions shape my beliefs and emotions.

A few years later tragedy touched down in my childhood church. My family had heard whispers of the scandal for months, and then one cloudy Sunday morning the pastor confirmed the rumors. He was having an affair with a woman on the worship team. Almost immediately, the couple ran off to another state and got married. The confession and runaway marriage ripped our church to pieces, breaking the faith of many in the congregation along with it.

At Sunday school the following week, I struggled to pay attention. I felt hurt, and I didn't know what to think or believe. The pastor who taught me the Bible had lied and cheated. How could this be happening, and what was I supposed to do?

A few of my friends came to me with tears in their eyes. "Our family is leaving the church," three of them told me. I wasn't surprised, but it still intensified the hurt. I knew their departure meant I'd most likely never see them again.

Later that night our family gathered together to talk about the affair.

"How can we trust the church anymore?" I asked my parents. "Lots of people are leaving...Maybe we should leave too."

"Oh, honey," my dad began, "the human condition is a broken condition. We are all flawed. That's just the reality of living here on earth. But you have to remember—the pastor isn't the church. He may have started the church, but he's just the pastor. The people are the church, and we can trust God and His Word. That's where our ultimate hope is. The pastor may have made a big mistake, but that doesn't negate the sermons he preached. Truth is truth, and all the rest, well, it's just noise."

Years later I asked my dad why he and my mom didn't leave the church.

"We just had to trust that God was in control of the situation. It was horribly messy and devastating, but we prayed about it and felt convicted to stay. So that's what we did," he said.

Between the singer's cancer diagnosis and the dilapidation of my home church after our pastor's affair, the weight of the world's brokenness hit my young faith like a bag of bricks. I began to see that outer appearances, social rankings, and titles do not matter when it comes to our broken, frail, and unreliable human condition. We all fall and we all bleed. And that was the first time I realized we were never meant to put all our faith, hope, and confidence in broken people, systems, or things. Doing so only leads to confusion, chaos, disappointment, and destruction—in our lives and in our world. And when our faith is misplaced, it's at a greater risk of being completely lost. I believe this early childhood experience and God's grace were a big part of the reason why I made it through the faith crisis I had in high school and college. Even to this day, when my health, mind, and strength fail me, I think back on these truths. And you know what?

Putting faith in things we cannot count on is a fool's errand, and the truth is that we can't count on much of anything in this world save for Jesus Christ.

The more I have clung to Jesus, the less confusing and chaotic my life has become.

The only solution to our brokenness and the only One worthy of our faith is God, who never fails. The world may fail us, but He never will.

There are several definitions for the word *fail*: "to lose strength, to fade or die away, to stop functioning normally, to fall short, to be inadequate, to be unsuccessful, to disappoint the expectations or trust of, to be deficient in, to leave undone"[9]—just to name a few. As I read these definitions, I wonder why anyone would want to put their faith in something that might fail. Seems pretty foolish, don't you think? And yet, how many of us have at one point or another put our faith in things other than God? If you were sitting across the table from me right now, you'd see me raising my hand. Yep, I'm guilty of putting my faith in things that fail. My health. Myself. My husband. My family. My friends. My calling.

I can tell you from experience that putting faith in things we cannot count on is a fool's errand, and the truth is that we can't count on much of anything in this world save for Jesus Christ. Everything that is happening in our world—senseless shootings, nuclear threats, political and racial discord, terrorist uprisings—should be proof that this is true, yet many of us can feel the tension in our souls. We're torn about what to believe. We don't know who we can trust. But there is still hope because faith that is misplaced or even lost can always be restored.

The Faith That's Worth Fighting For

From the dawn of creation to this very moment, one truth remains: *God is faithful and can be trusted.* Faith in what the media promote as the answer to our longing—the glamour of superstars or the prominence of those who are celebrated—does not fill our souls. But faith in God gives us the stability that the ever-changing voices of the world cannot. In this era of uncertainty, this is the faith that's worth fighting for.

Of course, a part of having faith is understanding and acknowledging God's existence and sovereignty, but to believe God exists is not enough. Even the demons "believe" in God and acknowledge his existence (James 2:19). That is only one piece of the puzzle. A deep and satisfying faith goes beyond acknowledging God to relying on Him in every area of life. This kind of faith doesn't just believe God exists; it puts faith into action by expressing confidence in who God says He is and what Jesus did on the cross.

Politicians and superstars may try to assert their authority and trustworthiness, but as is the case with every human being, eventually their words will betray them or be counted as false. Drugs, alcohol, food, cloth-ing, and other material pursuits, as noted earlier, can numb our pain for a little while, but their aid is only temporary. As someone who used sleep medication, TV shows, and food as coping mechanisms for years, I know this all too well. The reality of living in a broken world is that nothing can heal our hearts the way Jesus can, and every word we hear and everything we own will eventually fade away. What is considered "true" from a socie-tal standpoint now will not necessarily hold true for the future. Take views on fat, for example. Back in the 1990s, low-fat products were all the rage and fat was a diet no-no. In recent years, however, studies have revealed that it's really refined carbs we should be worried about.[10]

From the dawn of creation to this very moment, one truth remains: God is faithful and can be trusted.

If we know and understand that even the world's "experts" are constantly changing their minds about what is true, we must learn to stop grasping at temporary truths and stick with the truth that never changes—the Bible. The Bible was written by people who made mistakes but who loved God and knew that God's teachings were to be trusted and followed. Human thoughts, opinions, and claims can be wrong, but the Word of God is trustworthy and true.

I became convinced of this myself the more I started actually reading the Bible after my first counseling appointment. (Fun fact: I discovered the truth about fat and carbs in *TIME* magazine's "Ending the War on Fat" issue when I was in the waiting room for my counselor's appointment. I do not think this was by coincidence.) As I asked God to help me believe His Word for my life, He showed up to confirm what I was learning in count-less, unexplainable ways.

When we feel unsure of everything around us, faith in God's Word and the hope of swimming through the deep waters of life with Jesus are what sustain us. This faith is our stability in the waves. This faith is our hope and confidence. And this faith is our key to victory: "We are more than conquerors through him who loved us" (Romans 8:37). We are saved by faith, and we overcome by faith.

I'm passionate about a lot of things in life, but I don't know a better thing worth telling others about than this unfailing faith, because it has completely turned my life around! It has ushered me into the abundant life and freedom I dreamed about when I used to cry myself to sleep. Because of faith, I'm not waiting to live the abundant life in heaven; my eyes are open and I'm living in it here and now.

You see, faith has a transformative effect on every part of our lives. The reward of a faithful heart goes beyond the promise of heaven; there are blessings for this life, right now. When we fight for and step into faith, God's Word and His promises begin to unfold in our lives.

One of the biggest promises God fulfills in a person who fights for faith is the gift of the fruit of the Spirit. Unexplainable love, joy, peace, patience, kindness, goodness, faithfulness, gentleness, and self-control—this is what is available to us through faith in Jesus Christ. This is a gift the world cannot give.

In Mark 9:23 (CEB) Jesus says, "All things are possible for the one who has faith." By faith, we can accomplish the seemingly impossible. By faith, we can live beautiful, holy lives because God enables us to do so. No one exhibits this better than the apostle Paul. Though the Bible is full of stories that demonstrate faith's transformative power, Paul's story is the one I run to when I'm looking for inspiration.

Before his conversion, Paul—then called Saul—was known throughout the land for his attempts to destroy Christianity by persecuting Christians. How much did Paul hate Christians? Enough to speak murderous

When we fight for and step into faith, God's Word and His promises begin to unfold in our lives.

threats against the Lord's disciples (Acts 9:1) and stand by while a man was stoned to death for his faith (Acts 7:58). Not only did Paul himself not have faith in Jesus but he also made sure others wouldn't either—or they would be put to death.

But something incredible happened when the risen Jesus confronted Paul on his way to Damascus to persecute more Christians.

> As he was approaching Damascus on this mission, a light from heaven suddenly shone down around him. He fell to the ground and heard a voice saying to him, "Saul! Saul! Why are you persecuting me?"
>
> "Who are you, lord?" Saul asked.
>
> And the voice replied, "I am Jesus, the one you are persecuting! Now get up and go into the city, and you will be told what you must do." (Acts 9:3-6 NLT)

The light was so bright that it blinded Paul, but the men traveling with him helped him make it to Damascus (v. 8). Can you imagine what was going through Paul's mind? *I don't believe in God, but I just heard from Him—and now I'm blind.* Paul had every reason to turn around and run the other direction, but he didn't. And by going to Damascus, he took his first step of faith.

For three days Paul was blind and did not eat or drink (v. 9). But eventually Jesus sent a man named Ananias to restore Paul's sight (v. 17). A few days later, Paul was preaching that Jesus is the Son of God (v. 20). Now that's quite a transformation, don't you think?

When I read this story, I try to envision the leap it must have taken for Paul to go from persecuting Christians to preaching for the cause of Christ. In my imagination, the chasm is far too wide. The only way Paul could ever make that leap was for Jesus to make a way, and that way was through faith. Jesus gave Paul the strength to fight for faith in Him. He has done the same for me, and He can do it for you too.

Taking the Next Steps

Paul's story reminds us that we are always able and ready to act on the faith that is at work in our hearts to change us. Whether we've attended church since childhood or have not been in church for a while—or ever—even faith as small as a grain of mustard seed has the power to change us (Luke 17:6). But we must be willing to step out and say, "God, I may not trust You fully, but I'm going to choose faith over fear in this situation or area of my life; show me what You can do, and help me discover (or rediscover) You."

After having been diagnosed with hEDS, I've learned how to put this type of faith into practice almost every day as I work to manage my condition. What that looks like is choosing not to dwell on thoughts about surgery or ending up in a wheelchair. Instead, by faith I just keep putting one foot in front of the other and do what I can to honor the body God gave me.

I don't know if the physical therapy I do daily will keep my bones from degenerating more than they already have, but I'm trusting God to meet my needs and strengthen me as I look to Him to hold me together. Here's what I know beyond a shadow of a doubt: Fretting over where I'm going to be ten years, let alone five years, from now won't do me any good. But trusting God? Well, that has given me an indescribable peace unlike anything I've ever known.

Like Paul, when we live by faith we might feel that we are blind, swimming without sight of what's ahead; but Jesus is with us every step of the way, guiding us to where He wants us to be. Saying yes to God and following Jesus is a journey that we never walk alone. And when we say yes to putting our hope and trust in God, He promises to increase our faith: "For the eyes of the LORD range throughout the earth to strengthen those whose hearts are fully committed to him" (2 Chronicles 16:9).

So far we've seen that faith in Jesus is the answer to all of life's troubles, and that faith has the power to save us as long as we have the courage to reach out. Whether you're ready to take the next steps for the very first time or as a renewed commitment to a deeper faith, here are three things I suggest:

1. Renounce the worldly things you have put your faith in.
2. Acknowledge God's Word as the only reliable source of truth in your life (John 1:1-9) and make it a priority to study it often (Psalm 119:97, 105).
3. Recognize that you cannot and do not swim through life alone. God is our source of life, and He is also the source of our faith (Ephesians 2:8). Apart from Him, we have no good thing (Psalm 16:2). No peace. No joy. No hope.

Think about what you are putting your faith in today. Is it other people or your own efforts? Or have you lost faith like so many others in our world? Take some time to review the chapter and answer the questions below. Don't rush ahead to the next chapter before you've allowed God to work in your heart and reveal everything He wants to show you. Once you've taken a few moments to be honest with yourself, you'll be ready to move forward in this journey to a deeper faith.

GOING DEEPER

1. Have you ever tried to put your faith in something other than God? If so, what was the outcome?

2. Author Mark Batterson writes, "Faith is unlearning the senseless worries and misguided beliefs that keep us captive. It is far more complex than simply modifying behavior.... Faith is rewiring the human brain. Neurologically speaking, that is what we do when we study Scripture. We are literally upgrading our minds by downloading the mind of Christ."[11] What misguided beliefs are holding you captive? How does your mind need to be rewired today?

3. Romans 5:5 reminds us that "hope does not put us to shame, because God's love has been poured out into our hearts through the Holy Spirit, who has been given to us." Has this chapter made you feel more hopeful? If so, what are you more hopeful about?

4. Recall an experience when your faith in God was confirmed or strengthened. What did you learn from that experience that can encourage you to fight for faith today?

PRAYER

Jesus, thank You for the gift of faith. Thank You for not requiring me to have a mountain of faith in order to come to You. All I need is faith the size of a mustard seed for You to transform my life and keep me from drowning. Forgive me for putting my faith in broken people and broken things that can never save or satisfy my soul. Lord, help me have faith in You and You alone. May I hold steadfast to Your Word, which brings life. Fortify my faith right here, right now. Show me the power of a life surrendered in faith to You. I ask all these things in Jesus's holy name. Amen.

CHAPTER THREE

Six Things You Need to Know

When you go through deep waters,
I will be with you.

—Isaiah 43:2 NLT

I believe words have immeasurable power. That's why I'm a writer. That's why I strive to think long and hard about the words I choose before I write or say them. That's why I fight daily to speak life, love, hope, and truth over myself in order to drown out the cruel, untruthful things others have spoken over me. Words are powerful no matter what we are going through, but they are even more powerful when our faith is tested.

I wish I could forget some of the things people said to me when the waves of life came crashing in. "You're never going to get over this," they told me. "This is going to haunt you for the rest of your life." Or my personal favorite, "Do you have unresolved sin in your life? Maybe God is punishing you for something."

Maybe you can relate. Someone entered into your struggle and, instead of giving you a helping hand, shoved you further into the undercurrent. Whatever hurtful words and lies you've received over the years, there are six things you need to know before we move forward in our journey. Clinging to these truths helped me get through my crisis of faith and continues to help me navigate the deep with God each day.

1. God Is Not Punishing You

Punishment is incompatible with the gospel of Jesus Christ. In the Book of Hebrews we read, "For by one sacrifice he has made perfect forever those who are being made holy....And where these have been forgiven, sacrifice for sin is no longer necessary" (10:14, 18). The gospel says that because of Christ's sacrifice, our sins have been forgiven and forgotten: "If we confess our sins, He is faithful and righteous to forgive us our sins and to cleanse us from all unrighteousness (1 John 1:9 NASB). Jesus's death and resurrection paid all our debts and freed us from the power and penalty of sin.

So when we suffer, we can know that it is not for our punishment but for a greater purpose. The Scriptures tell us that God does not cause suffering but allows it, not to torment us or obliterate our hope but to

- redeem it for our good, drawing us to full reliance on Him (2 Corinthians 1:8-9);
- develop our character as we become more righteous and holy (Romans 5:3-5);

- increase our capacity to comfort and encourage others (2 Corinthians 1:3-5);
- show His grace, power, and glory to the world (2 Corinthians 12:9; John 9:3); and
- manifest the life and character of Christ in the midst of suffering (2 Corinthians 4:8-12; 1 Peter 3:14-17).

This is why testimonies of believers who have walked through suffering are so powerful (and why I've written a whole chapter on testimonies to round out this book). When we are weak, Christ is strong; and that makes a powerful statement to the world about the God we love and follow.

Sufferings and trials serve a purpose in our lives and the lives of everyone around us. While we may never know why God allows something painful to happen to us, we can trust Him to work all things together for the good—not the punishment—of those who love him (Romans 8:28).

2. You're Not Alone

Of all the hurtful words we could ever latch on to, the lie that we are alone might be the deadliest. It also could not be further from the truth of the Scriptures. Deuteronomy 31:6 clearly states that God is always with us and will never leave or forsake us, and Jesus himself said, "And surely I am with you always, to the very end of the age" (Matthew 28:20).

When we take a step back and look at those around us, it can be easy to think we're the only ones who don't have it together. At times we might even tell ourselves, *No one could be as messed up as me.* But the reality is, "all have sinned and fall short of the glory of God" (Romans 3:23). And because of our sin, we all suffer in different ways. Just because someone seems to have a perfect life doesn't mean that it is. Take business executives, for example. They may receive higher salaries and wear nicer clothes, but behind closed doors they could be drowning in anxiety, anger, depression, addiction, or some other sin. We can never truly know what someone else is going through until we get to know that person.

For years I drifted through life believing that I was alone in my struggle with physical pain, anxiety, and depression and that everyone else was better off. I kept my suffering to myself, but the isolation only multiplied my pain. Things changed when I allowed myself to be vulnerable enough to share my story with others. And you know what happened? The more I shared my story, the more the walls of shame that the enemy of my soul had built around me started to crumble. To this day, as I continue to struggle with physical and mental health flare-ups, I know that sharing my story is part of what keeps the enemy from dragging me back to the pit that God rescued me from. And I see how my willingness to be vulnerable has ministered and brought hope to others, which is a joy in itself.

Scripture tells us that the enemy is the father of lies and an accuser (John 8:44; Revelation 12:10). He wants us to feel like we're alone so that we will doubt the promises of God, but we would be wise not to let him shame us in this way. These days when I hear the accuser's lies, I immediately refute them. I remind myself that there are others who also are enduring painful circumstances, and even if no one on earth could relate to what I'm going through, I serve a High Priest who understands every heartache and every tear (Hebrews 4:15).

Beloved, you are not alone. You never have been and never will be.

3. You're Going to Be OK

Even the fiercest storms have an expiration date.

As I am writing these words, we have just witnessed the most intense hurricane season in more than a decade. First, Hurricane Harvey hit Houston. Less than one month later, Hurricane Irma struck the Caribbean and

Florida. And just two weeks after that, Hurricane Maria ravaged Puerto Rico and the Caribbean.

Irma was one the strongest and costliest Atlantic basin hurricanes ever recorded, and its winds devastated the eastern Caribbean nations and territories, damaging more than 70 percent of the buildings there. My friend Marva and her family were four of the more than 200,000 people there who found themselves needing aid after the Category 5 hurricane decimated everything in its path.[1]

In a matter of days, Marva and her family went from living a normal life in paradise to having to leave their own country for health concerns. Today Marva and her two children have relocated to the States while her husband remains in the Caribbean for work. The couple is praying for God to open doors for their family to be together, but much about the future is still unknown. And yet just as the winds of Hurricane Irma eventually settled, they are trusting God to settle this storm too. They are choosing to focus not on today's troubles but on the hope of a better tomorrow.

Marva's story reminds me of the hope mentioned in 2 Corinthians 4:18, where the apostle Paul reminds us of the truth that what is seen is temporary but what is unseen is eternal. When life becomes chaotic, it's easy to focus on the waves threatening to take us out. But the waves are only temporary. They will die down eventually. And through it all, the Word of God is what endures (Psalm 119:89)—not the storm.

Every time I have a long stretch of bad pain days or my brain feels like it's off-kilter again, I remind myself that better days are ahead of me and having a bad day doesn't mean I have a bad life.

Beloved, I know what it's like to stare into the future and wonder if you'll ever smile, laugh, or dance again. If that's you today—if you are tired—remember that hope is never lost. Look beyond the waves. Hear me when I say you're going to be OK. The saying is really true: this too shall pass. Whatever you are facing is not the end of your story. You will live to see another day. And that's not a cliché—it's a promise.

I don't know what your future holds any more than I know what Marva's future or my own future holds, but I do know this: with Jesus on our side, we're not only going to be OK; we're going to be way better than OK!

4. Darkness Does Not Define You

Last year I woke up in the middle of a nightmare with a traumatic flashback fresh in my mind from those dreadful high school and college days.[2] My heart was racing, my chest was tight, and my body was drenched in sweat. I tried to shove the memories playing in my head to the side, but I couldn't shake the feeling of sheer panic. In my delirium I struggled to catch a breath and got up to splash some water on my face.

The cold water refreshed me as it washed away my beads of sweat, but seconds later I felt tears taking their place.

Usually I would have stopped the waterworks from getting out of control. You know, stuff the tears back where they came from. But this time, as they rolled down my cheek, I didn't try to stop them. Like a rushing river I just let them flow.

With Jesus on our side, we're not only going to be OK; we're going to be way better than OK!

I looked at myself in the mirror and scowled. What's wrong with you? Seriously . . . you're pathetic. You should be ashamed of yourself right now, I thought to myself.

I knew these thoughts were lies from the enemy, but the longer I stared at myself, the more I started to consider them. Sure, there is always hope in Jesus, but part of me felt hopeless, like a Humpty-Dumpty who could never be put back together again. Darkness and trials have a way of making us question who we really are.

If you're familiar with any of the Star Wars movies, you've heard of the Force. There's the Living Force (as in Yoda and Obi-Wan Kenobi), but there is also a Dark Side of the Force (the Sith and Darth Vader). Here's the thing: Vader didn't always belong to the Dark Side.

Like so many of us he began his journey as an innocent, wide-eyed child of the light named Anakin Skywalker. But somewhere along the way the darkness found him, and Anakin quickly became lost and confused. Fight though he might against the dark, the battle made him forget who he really was.

Friend, we too face a similar battle every day. There is an enemy. There is darkness. And our enemy will do everything he can to blindside us and steal our joy and identity in Christ.

On the night of my flashback last year, I was blindsided by my past— by something I thought I'd dealt with but was bubbling up once again. The darkness found me and the enemy was trying to beat me down.

But I know better.

Deep in my soul I know the Jesus inside me is stronger than the darkness that threatens to overtake me.

I also know who I am.

I am a child of God. A child of the light and of the day. A child with 24/7 access to joy, love, peace, hope, and the power of the Holy Spirit. A child whose heavenly Father loves her no matter what. A child who can face the darkness because the light inside her can help her overcome anything.

You see, there is a darkness but we don't belong to it. Not only do we not belong to it, it also has no authority over us.

Friend, I don't know what darkness you may be struggling with in this season. But whatever you're facing, I want you to know that the darkness does not control or define you.

There was a time in my life when I let my struggles define me, but I'm not going back there—to the darkness, to the night, to the overwhelming pit of despair. And neither are you. Because we have been called into the light—into a life of courageous faith. And we don't have to even entertain the darkness because as children of God it's not who we are. It does not define us. Say it with me: *The darkness does not define me.*

5. You Were Made for the Deep

As a water lover, I'm partial to anything ocean related, so you can imagine my excitement when the computer-animated film *Moana* finally hit Netflix. (Yes, I still love animated movies—and c'mon, who doesn't?) Shortly after its debut, I snuggled into our living room couch with a huge bowl of buttery popcorn, ready to discover what everyone had been raving about.

Though, for me, nothing can ever come close to *Finding Nemo* or *The Little Mermaid*, *Moana* exceeded my expectations and gave me goosebumps from head to toe. Underneath the fictional Hawaiian demigod narrative is a beautiful story about a girl who longs to venture past the shoreline—beyond the reef and into the deep.

The Jesus inside me is stronger than the darkness that threatens to overtake me.

I don't believe the timing of me watching *Moana* as I was preparing to write this chapter was accidental. I had prayed in faith for guidance, and suddenly I found God speaking to me through a Disney movie. If that isn't proof that God can use anything to speak to us, I don't know what is!

There's a scene in *Moana* that encapsulates everything about the journey to a deeper faith—the very journey we are embarking on together through this book—and I want to share it with you in the hopes that it will stir your heart the same way it stirred mine. While the movie deals with demigod spirituality, I think the overarching elements tie into the struggles we can encounter in our own Christian faith. If you've seen the movie, perhaps my retelling will help you see it in a new light.

We meet Moana on the island of Motunui, where she has grown up with great wealth, privilege, and status as the daughter of a chief. Whatever Moana needs, she can get from the island. She doesn't have a reason to leave the safety of the shoreline. Yet no matter what season of life Moana finds herself in, she isn't satisfied hanging out on the land or in the shallows. She longs to go deeper and explore the sea, even if it means falling into danger along the way.

Moana's desire for the deep comes to a head in the chorus of the movie's hit single, "How Far I'll Go":

> See the line where the sky meets the sea? It
> calls me...
> One day I'll know, if I go there's just no
> telling how far I'll go.[3]

This calling or longing is what propels Moana to finally sail beyond the reef despite her culture's fear of the ocean.

Though her journey is fraught with storms, battles, and many disasters to overcome, it's clear as the story unfolds that Moana has made the right choice. Without giving too much of the movie away, let's just say that if Moana had stayed on Motunui where things were seemingly secure, she and the entire island would have fallen into greater peril than the ocean ever could cause. And so, though fear initially has kept Moana from embarking on the adventure, courage and faith help her overcome in the end.

Do you see the parallels between Moana and the adventure to a deeper faith you and I are embarking on together? When we step out in faith, we do not always know where God will take us. But we will never know how far we can go or how much we can accomplish if we do not take courage and embrace the deep in faith. Our faith can take us further than we ever dreamed we could go. Never in a million years did I imagine I'd be writing books or hosting a podcast and national women's events, but that's the beauty of following where God leads. As we say yes to His leading and commit our plans to Him, I've experienced that God is eager and able to exceed our earthly expectations of what we can do for His Kingdom.

God is eager and able to exceed our earthly expectations of what we can do for His Kingdom.

That's the beauty and mystery of the deep—of this adventure called faith—and it's in this adventure that we have the chance to experience miracles in the midst of impossible circumstances.

I don't know about you, but I want to see miracles and wonders. I want to see God move as never before. And if that means never going back to the shallow end where things are seemingly secure, well, that's fine by me.

The story of Moana makes me think about the story of Moses and the Israelites in Exodus 14, when they stood before the Red Sea as Pharaoh and the Egyptians threatened to overtake them. Can you imagine the thoughts that might have been going through the Israelites' heads when Moses told them to leave the safety of the shoreline and venture into the deep? My best guess is that they went something like this: *Are you crazy? Don't you see there is a raging sea in front of us? I'm not walking out into that water. No siree. You can go ahead and let yourself drown out there, but I didn't sign up for this level of insanity.*

But the God who calls us to step out in faith always makes a way for us to journey through the deep with Him. With Moses leading the way, that's what the Israelites were about to see for themselves: "Then Moses stretched out his hand over the sea, and all that night the LORD drove the sea back with a strong east wind and turned it into dry land. The waters were divided, and the Israelites went through the sea on dry ground, with a wall of water on their right and on their left" (Exodus 14:21-22).

In this miraculous moment in history, God not only led His people safely through the sea but He also used the same waters to crush the Egyptians, as we read just a few verses later. Exodus 14:28 tells us that not one of them survived. And so the same waters the Israelites thought would kill them ended up saving them. Much like Moana, had Moses failed to exercise courage and faith, the Israelites would have been defeated.

I get chills every time I read the end of Exodus 14: "When the people of Israel saw the mighty power that the LORD had unleashed against the Egyptians, they were filled with awe before him. They put their faith in the LORD and in his servant Moses" (v. 31 NLT).

Did you catch that last sentence? They put their faith in the Lord and in Moses. Surely the Israelites had to exercise a little bit of faith in order to walk across the sea, but when I look at this passage of Scripture in context, I can't help wondering if their actions were *predominantly* fueled by fear. Think about it: if thousands of warriors were about to kill you and your loved ones and an escape route presented itself, you'd probably head toward the flashing Exit sign to avoid annihilation, right? If we take time to read all of Exodus 14, we notice there is no talk of the Israelites trusting God as they journeyed through the Red Sea—save for Moses, of course. It was only after they had made it through the trial that they chose to put all their faith and trust in God and in Moses.

The application for us is this: we were made for the deep, and that's exactly where God wants to meet us and multiply our faith—whether we find ourselves there by choice, like Moana, or by circumstance, like the Israelites. Either way, we don't have to be afraid because our God is always with us. He's the wind in our sail, taking us out into the deep for a great adventure.

What Red Sea are you dealing with today? Are you standing on the shoreline or swimming out in the middle of it? Regardless of where you are, how is God calling you to exercise faith? Maybe it's by trusting that you aren't going to drown and that God will rescue you. Maybe it's by going to church for the first time in years. Maybe it's by trusting God to provide for your family even though you just lost your job. Maybe it's trusting God for healing, whether it comes on this side of heaven or not. Or maybe God has placed a call on your life—to serve in your community, to love a family member who betrayed you, to go on mission for God. You may be scared of what swimming into the unknown could mean for you, but like Moana and Moses, you cannot deny the call.

What is your Red Sea, your deep water? Are you willing to jump in?

6. God's Love Will Carry You

One of my favorite places to vacation is a resort on an island in the Bahamas. My husband and I always joke with each other, saying that if we came into a lot of money, we would give the majority of it away and then stay at the resort until the money ran out. Judging by the fact that a slice of pizza goes for twelve dollars there, this might not seem like the wisest investment. But if you've been somewhere as beautiful as this place, you might agree it's worth every penny.

I owe my love and appreciation for this island resort to my sweet mother-in-law, who was generous enough to take my husband and me there. If it weren't for her, I may never have experienced the wonders of the aquariums, beaches, pools, lazy river, water slides, and dining halls. Of all these wonders, the lazy river remains my attraction of choice.

Imagine sitting in the middle of a big, blue inflatable tube as a slow, serene current carries you down a crystal clear river. The sun is high in the sky and you look up to bask your face in its warmth for a while. Sounds pretty blissful, right?

What I didn't realize the first time I took a turn in the lazy river was that it's not exactly tame. It wasn't until after we traveled home and I looked at online videos to relive the experience that I discovered its nickname, the Lazy (Crazy) River. If you ask me, the nickname aptly describes it. One minute the current is relaxing and you don't even have to hold on to the inflatable, and then BAM! The current picks up out of nowhere, sending you into a series of rocky rapids.

Watching videos from other tourists made me realize how rough the currents really were, but also how dangerous things could have been without a tube. I certainly wouldn't want to go through such turbulence without having something to hold me up. Knowing how uncoordinated I am, I'd probably end up with a concussion, or worse.

This is how navigating the deep waters of life can be. The seas might be calm for a little while, but eventually things will pick up again, and eventually the waves will become too much for us to handle on our own. While God doesn't cause the waves, He graciously offers us a choice: Will we reach out for Him and enter the currents of His love, or sink into the undercurrents of despair? The first choice brings life; the second brings death.

Can I tell you a secret? Sometimes I feel unworthy of God's love. In the past, those feelings of unworthiness kept me from reaching out to Him. I was ashamed, and I allowed my shame to lead me down a despairing path.

Fortunately for you and me, God's love is the kind that pursues and chases us down until we let it in. Nothing can keep us from His love; and after decades of watching Him chase after me, I can tell you that there is no greater love. But don't just take my word for it. Read what Romans 8:35-39 has to say:

> Who shall separate us from the love of Christ? Shall trouble or hardship or persecution or famine or nakedness or danger or sword? As it is written:
>
> > "For your sake we face death all day long;
> > we are considered as sheep to be slaughtered."
>
> No, in all these things we are more than conquerors through him who loved us. For I am convinced that neither death nor life, neither angels nor demons, neither the present nor the future, nor any powers, neither height nor depth, nor anything else in all creation, will be able to separate us from the love of God that is in Christ Jesus our Lord.

I don't know about you, but knowing I was made for the deep is not enough. I don't just want to survive; I want to thrive! I don't want to be submerged by life-threatening, soul-crushing waters; I want to be submerged in God's love—a love that will carry me and see me through. I don't want to fight the waves on my own; I want to let Jesus take over as He clears my lungs and floods my heart with His love, joy, grace, power, and perfect peace.

Let's apply this concept of two different kinds of currents to the story of Moses who, like many of us, was called into the deep and challenged to exercise faith. As he led the Israelites out of Egypt, crossing the threshold from the shore to the waters of the Red Sea posed many dangers and fears. But when troubles surfaced, Moses pressed into faith; and as a result, God's people did not sink into the undercurrents of despair. Instead, Moses's courage and faith sustained the Israelites in the deep as Moses held on to what he knew to be true—that God loved them and could be trusted, no matter what.

God is the fountain of living water (Jeremiah 2:13; John 7:38), so if we're going to drown in anything when we put our faith in Him, it's not going to be the undercurrents of despair but the currents of His love. His perfect, unfailing love will carry us!

As I shared earlier, I spent much of my life caught in the undercurrents of despair before I put my faith in Jesus. I didn't know how to break free from my captivity, and so I closed myself off from receiving God's love. I heard people say His love was strong enough to save me, but after years of battling the same issues and seeing little to no progress, I had hardened my heart to the truth.

I can't pinpoint the moment when God's love finally broke through my incomprehension. It's not as if I woke up one morning and instantly felt God's love. Instead, much like my unraveling, recognizing and accepting God's love was a process. The more I prayed for God to reveal and help me feel His love, the more He showed up in the most amazing ways to woo me back to Him. I do not have enough pages here to tell you the ways in which God has demonstrated His great love for me, but I will tell you this: the depths of His great love saved and continue to save me from sinking into despair.

There's a song I listen to on my morning prayer walks, and the lyrics are part of what God used to inspire me as I was writing this book. The song is titled "Into the Deep," but interestingly God gave me the name for the book before this song took hold of my heart. I encourage you to find the song online and listen to it after you've read this chapter, but for now I want to share these lines:

> Into the deep I will go with You
> Submerge my feet to my head in all of You[4]

This is what we were made for: to drown in God's love—not in the world's despair. And the deep waters—the unknown—is where His love abounds.

If the waves are raging around you right now, remember: God is not punishing you; you're not alone; you're going to be OK; darkness does not define you; you were made for the deep; and God's love will carry you.

GOING DEEPER

1. Can you think of a time when you were called to have faith or take a risk? How did that calling make you feel?
2. What fears are keeping you from stepping out in faith or taking a risk now? Have you expressed those fears to God?
3. Read Exodus 14. If you were one of the Israelites, how do you think you would have reacted to the parting of the Red Sea? What would you have done if you were in their shoes?
4. What would it look like for God to part and calm the waters in your life?
5. Our understanding of God's love impacts our ability to trust Him. When you think about God's love for you, what images, thoughts, or feelings come to mind? Where or how do you think you learned to have this understanding of God?
6. Do you believe God's love is strong enough to save you from the waves in your life? If not, what is keeping you from believing and accepting His love? If yes, how could choosing to swim in the currents of God's love, rather than in the undercurrents of despair, change your life?

PRAYER

Precious Father, thank You for your presence and Your love. Thank You for calling me into the deep—where my feet may fail but You never will. I am so grateful that I don't have to be afraid of the waters raging around me, because that's where You call me and meet me. Help me keep my eyes fixed on You, trading my deep despair for deep faith in You. Keep my heart from giving in to the undercurrents of despair, and drown me in the currents of Your love. Multiply my faith today as I reach out for You. In Jesus's name. Amen.

CHAPTER FOUR

Trusting God in the Deep

Faith is not believing in my own unshakable belief.
Faith is believing an unshakable God when
everything in me trembles and quakes.

—*Beth Moore*[1]

Every night after dinner, Alex and I take a walk around our neighborhood or the local park. Sometimes we keep our words to a minimum and use the time to clear our heads, but most of our walks are full of conversation. As two incredibly driven and passionate human beings, we love to dream together. We're always looking for a new adventure—always working toward a new goal.

It's common for us to brainstorm on our nightly walks as our beloved fur baby, Reese, walks with us. But the frequency of our conversations about dreams didn't keep me from being caught off guard one night when Alex blurted out of the blue: "I want to buy a business, and I think that's what God is calling me to do."

The news hit me like a huge tidal wave and knocked me off my feet. All I could think was, *Whoa, hold the phone! What is going on?*

"You want to do what?" I replied, stopping to lock eyes with him before we continued walking down the sidewalk.

I knew Alex had an entrepreneurial spirit from the moment we met. During our first summer together, he started his own neighborhood mulching business. Two months later, he also launched a multimedia company to meet local audiovisual needs. His grandfather and uncle were business owners, and his dad was a top-performing salesman. Business was in his blood. But that didn't make the reality of his dream easy to swallow. All passion and experience aside, buying a business comes with a lot of risks, and I wasn't sure if I was ready for those risks.

Later that night, the practical side of me made a list of the pros and cons of small-business ownership. I still had a lot of reservations after putting my thoughts and emotions on paper, but one pro stood out enough to conquer all the cons: *You can trust Alex.*

I couldn't trust the business acquisition to go smoothly and be profitable from day one. I couldn't trust that the government or other people would always support small businesses. I couldn't trust our finances to be solid for the rest of our lives. I couldn't trust the location of where we'd end up moving or how long it would be before we settled into a house again. But after eight years of doing life together, I knew Alex's character. I'd taken a chance on him and given him my heart in high school, and over time he had proven himself faithful to me. I knew I could trust him to do what was best for us. I could trust that when the man I love said he believed this was what he was called to do, he meant it. I just had to be willing to let go of control and surrender the situation to God and to Alex.

Holding on to earthly things—such as our jobs, relationships, health, and schedules—creates stress. But letting go? Beloved, there's freedom in surrender.

The same principles apply to putting our trust in God and surrendering our lives to Him. We must deeply know and trust Him if we are ever going to experience freedom in Him, which begs the question: *can God really be trusted, and if so, what steps can we take to surrender our lives to Him more and more each day?* This is the question we'll explore together in this chapter.

Trust Takes Time

While there is some logic behind our ability to trust, most of our decision-making is based on the emotions we feel toward someone and the time we've spent cultivating a relationship with that person. Trust is a choice, and in every relationship we have two options: do we allow ourselves to be fully available, vulnerable, and transparent, or do we put up walls and shut the person out? With so many factors and emotions to consider, it makes sense that trust doesn't come easily for a lot of us. Many people struggle to trust freely, easily, or fully—myself included.

Layer on top of that being burned or deeply hurt by someone, and trust can feel unnatural if not impossible at times. While working on this book, Alex and I experienced a huge test of faith. One day everything was coming up roses in our lives, and the next day I came home to a letter full of damaging accusations and threats. My heart hurt when the false accusations continued to come at us. I didn't know what God wanted me to do, so I did the only thing I could do: pray, wait, and trust. In the end, my husband and I knew we couldn't trust this person's unpredictable behavior. Instead, we chose to trust God in the decision we felt Him leading us to make. And as hard as that decision was, we are trusting Him to continue to bring beauty out of the ashes of that battle.

The reason I am able to trust God today is because I've spent the last ten years asking Him to help me trust Him more. Trust still isn't always my first instinct when a new crisis bubbles up, but the more I actively choose to trust God, the easier it has become to surrender my circumstances to Him and let Him work things out (versus me striving in my own strength to make things work out).

Our decision to trust is made easier when people have proven themselves worthy of our trust by being consistently honest, respectable, and dependable. But this requires time on our part. We have to be willing to give others time if they are going to have a chance to prove themselves to us.

If we want to trust God, we must let go of control and spend quality time discovering who He really is.

That's why it was so easy for me to trust Alex's decision to buy a business. At the time, he had an eight-year track record of being nothing but truthful and reliable. I honestly don't think the man has ever told me a lie. And it's hard for me to imagine that he ever would, because that has not been his character. While these things are true, I wouldn't know this about Alex if I hadn't spent time getting to know him—what he loves, what he values, what he is like. Trust takes time—with people and with God.

We admire people who seem to trust God freely, easily, and fully. We wish we could doubt less and trust more. Yet if we examine our lives, the truth is that we spend more time dwelling on our doubts than we spend surrendering and pressing into God.

I wonder how many of us feel that we can't trust God, yet we've never given Him a chance to prove Himself worthy of our trust. We've never let Him show us just how faithful and good He really is because we're too caught up in trying to do everything ourselves. If we want to trust God, we must let go of control and spend quality time discovering who He really is.

Hello, My Name Is Miss Control Freak

When I think about how quality time affects a relationship's overall value and level of trust, I am challenged to be honest about my own struggles with trusting God. If I think about it, I am painfully aware of how fragile and conditional my faith has been since I first pursued a relationship with Jesus as a child. When I think back to those high school and college days when my faith was at its weakest, I cringe, because in hindsight, I see those were also the moments when I pushed God away. I wonder what would have happened if I'd drawn closer to Him in those moments instead.

The truth is, my fleshly response to a crisis is to waffle between trusting God fully and trusting myself more than I trust God. This is especially true for the little things in life. Trusting Him with the big things is easy. I have faith that He created this earth and everything on it. I have no doubt that He created me to fulfill a unique purpose. I believe He is sovereign—all-powerful and above all things. But there are seasons in my life when my beliefs struggle to make their way from my head to my heart, because at my core I tend to value control more than I value trust.

I love control. I crave it. I relish it. I look for ways to have more of it.

If being a control freak isn't bad enough, I've lived my entire life in a culture that exalts self-efficiency, self-esteem, and self-confidence. So even today it can be hard for me to trust God with the little things—the things I think I can manage better on my own, such as my relationships, goals, and schedule. If I'm completely honest, my default is to trust myself more than I trust God in these smaller areas.

From this place of half-trust, it's as if I'm saying: OK, God, I know You're real, but with You being invisible and all…part of me isn't 100 percent certain You're going to come through this time. So I'll go ahead and handle this one. You can go back to doing whatever You do. I'll take it from here.

I know God is good. I know God is for me and is working all things together for my good. On the other hand, sometimes it's just easier to trust myself to get things done rather than sit around and wait for Him to make a move.

But I don't want to half-trust God! I want to *fully* trust Him every single day of my life. I want to relinquish all control to Him. And when it seems that I can't, that my flesh wants to hold on to control and keep doing everything myself, I have found there is only one way to resolve my trust issues: I have to go back to the basics as I did when I was learning to fully trust Him—back to spending quality time with God, remembering His character, and resting in His faithful track record—because relationships take time, and surrendering control is the only way to cultivate trust.

Relationships take time, and surrendering control is the only way to cultivate trust.

Pushing God away and trying to do things by ourselves won't help us learn to trust Him, but surrendering control and spending time getting to know Him will.

Getting to Know God

Many parents have to force their children to go to church, but I was always the first family member in the car on Sunday mornings. "Hurry up! Hurry up! Hurry up!" I'd shout to my sister, mom, and dad before running out to the garage. I loved going to church for three main reasons: food, fellowship, and fun. And if you've ever attended one of the *She Found Joy* events that I host, then you know I'm still as passionate about those three things today.

Each week while our parents sat in the regular worship service, we went to Sunday school where we sang songs, learned new stories from the Bible, and played games with friends. Usually the food the leaders provided was a simple snack, such as apple slices, popcorn, pretzels, or celery sticks with peanut butter. But every now and then they treated us to pizza and cookies.

On pizza Sundays, all the kids swarmed like bees to form a line the second the delivery person entered the building. Because budging in line was frowned upon at church, wherever you landed in line determined what kind of pizza you ate. If you were at the front of the line, you could guarantee yourself a slice of pepperoni or veggie pizza. But if you were at the back of the line, you probably were going to get stuck with sausage or cheese. When I didn't make it to the front of the line, I'd say a little prayer for God to leave me a slice of pepperoni: "Pretty, pretty please, God."

After we grabbed our pizza and chocolate chip cookies, our leaders guided us in a prayer we knew by heart: "God is great, God is good, and we thank Him for our food." It's a standard childhood prayer, and if you grew up going to church or saying grace at the family table, you've probably recited these same words multiple times.

While there's nothing inherently wrong with this prayer, part of me wonders if some of us never move past this elementary, shallow-end portrayal of God. We think the idea of Him is great, and we appreciate His help (not to mention the delicious food He blesses us with), but that's about all we know about Him. He's there, and He blesses people. Yay, God!

I don't know about you, but if my faith was floundering, that argument alone would not be enough to make me trust God. After all, I need more when it comes to trusting people. I don't care if someone's a good person; I want proof. I'm talking hard evidence here, especially if I haven't known the person very long. I need to know about his or her history. In the same way, I need to know more about God if I'm going to trust Him fully.

Here's the good news: God is not some distant being off in outer space. He's a personal God, and He designed us to be in relationship with Him. He wants us to *know* Him! He is El Shaddai, Adonai, Yahweh, Jehovah Jireh, Jehovah Shalom, and El Olam. He is Savior, Father, and Friend. He is holy, merciful, loving, powerful, faithful, unchanging, omniscient, just, righteous, compassionate, gracious, patient, perfect, wise, true, and basically any other positive adjective we could come up with. God is all these things and more.

When life is hard or I've simply fallen away from spending time with God, these two charts help me remember all the reasons why I can trust God. I developed these charts during a trial I experienced a few years ago. They can be a good reference for you, too, when you need to remember the nature and character of God so that you can trust Him more.

The names of God remind me who He truly is:

Adonai	Lord, Master (Genesis 15:2)
El Elyon	The Most High God (Genesis 14:18-20)
El Olam	The Everlasting God (Isaiah 40:28-31)
El Roi	The God Who Sees (Genesis 16:13)
El Shaddai	God Almighty (Genesis 17:1)
Elohim	God of Power and Might (Genesis 1:1)
Jehovah Jireh	The Lord Will Provide (Genesis 22:13-14)
Jehovah Mekoddishkem	The Lord Who Sanctifies You (Exodus 31:13)
Jehovah Nissi	The Lord My Banner/Victory (Exodus 17:15)
Jehovah Raah	The Lord My Shepherd (Psalm 23:1)

Jehovah Rapha	The Lord Who Heals (Exodus 15:26)
Jehovah Sabaoth	The Lord of Hosts (Isaiah 1:24)
Jehovah Shalom	The Lord Is Peace (Judges 6:24)
Jehovah Shammah	The Lord Is There/Present (Ezekiel 48:35)
Jehovah Tsidkenu	The Lord Our Righteousness (Jeremiah 23:6)
Yahweh	Lord, Jehovah (Deuteronomy 6:4)
Jesus	Savior; The Way, The Truth & The Life; Prince of Peace; The Good Shepherd; The Vine; The Bread of Life; The Light of the World; God with Us

The attributes of God remind me that He can be trusted:

Holy	Isaiah 6:3
Merciful	Ephesians 2:4-5
Gracious	Ephesians 2:8-9
Loving	1 John 4:7-10
Omniscient	Psalm 139:1-6
Wise	Proverbs 3:19-20
Faithful	Psalm 89:1-8; Psalm 119:90; 2 Timothy 2:13
Good	Psalm 119:65-72
Patient	2 Peter 3:9
Unchanging	Hebrews 13:8
Powerful	1 Corinthians 6:14
Mighty to Save	Zephaniah 3:17

Seasons change, people disappoint us, jobs come and go, and we all make mistakes. But God? He is unlike anyone or anything else on this earth, and that's why we can trust Him. He cannot change (Hebrews 13:8; James 1:17), disappoint, or make mistakes. It's not in His nature. For God to be anything other than what His Word declares Him to be...well, that would be like me eating 10,000 hamburgers—totally impossible!

This world will beat us down, but never forget that our God is still a good God. He is for redemption. He is for healing. He is for restoration. Everything else, whether it's despair, depression, hopelessness, or doubt—that's what the father of lies is for. But the good news for us is that God reigns victorious over the enemy. The battle is already won. So, the question is not a matter of who is going to win but a matter of who will have the courage to put their trust in God and claim the victory for themselves.

Raising the White Flag

I don't believe in reincarnation, but there's a running joke among some of my family members that in another life I was a NASCAR driver. I live for speed. When my grandparents gave me the keys to their 1988 Corvette the summer before my senior year of high school, I thought I had died and gone to automobile heaven. You may laugh, but I have a dream where one day I'm driving that red Corvette on the autobahn in Germany. Did you know that the speed record on this highway is 268.9 miles per hour, set by the German racing driver Rudolph Caracciola on January 29, 1938?[2] Insanity, I know, but if he were alive and he asked me to sit in the passenger seat, I would gladly oblige.

Since street racing is illegal here in the states, I'm content to settle for a good go-kart race every now and then. When Alex and I met, we'd go to the track a few times a year; but now that we're married, our trips have become less frequent, making my desire to win that much stronger. If you want to see sparks fly, just come to a go-kart race between Alex and me. We mean business and don't mess around.

At one of our first go-karting rendezvous, the track supervisor positioned us at the back of the pack. *Great, I'm already behind*, I thought to myself. But before I had a chance to mull over my race strategy, he waved the green flag, and off we went. After I adjusted to the car's handling on the first lap, every subsequent lap turned into a fight to pass more people and make it to the front of the pack. I pushed my foot as hard as I could into the accelerator. I took tight turns. I hit a few bumpers to throw people off track. But no matter what I did, I still couldn't make it to the front. And then I saw it. The white flag. The final lap. Time to surrender.

A white flag can have a negative connotation for many of us, especially if we aren't in the position we want to be in when it is raised. When the white flag came out on the go-kart track, I wanted to be in a position of power—at least first or second place, and I think that's how a lot of us feel about life. We want to overcome, reach the finish line on our own accord, and be recognized for our victory. We want to raise a white flag only if it means we come out on top. But that's not the kind of life God has called us to. Instead, we are to:

> Be still before the LORD
> and wait patiently for him;
> do not fret when people succeed in their ways.
> (Psalm 37:7)

God is the Victorious One. Only He is worthy of that first-place prize. And the rest of us? We have the joy of being able to rest in His victory—to raise our white flag and surrender our lives to the One who is able to give victory to all, regardless of where we are.

There is freedom in surrender, in raising our white flag from the very start. Instead of fretting about every twist, turn, and outcome, we can live uninhibited because we know that ultimately God is in control. He is good, and He will help us make it to where we are supposed to go.

I wasn't willing to relinquish control during that go-kart race, but God gave me another chance to exercise surrender a few years later on my wedding day. By this point in life, I had seen enough movies and had been in enough weddings to know that trying to control every little detail of a wedding day only led to chaos, heartache, and disappointment. The only things on my to-do list for October 12, 2014, were to honor God, marry Alex, have fun, and not be a bridezilla.

It didn't matter that my sister woke me up at 4 a.m. after having an allergic reaction to a medication she had taken. It didn't matter that I couldn't go back to sleep and went to sit in the hot tub at my gym instead. It didn't matter that the wind was blowing like a hurricane and messed up some of our pictures. It didn't matter that the reception venue vetoed my hanging decorations. I had learned that I'm not in control of everything, and I knew that trying to control any of those things would be a futile effort. The only thing I could control was saying "I do" to the love of my life. I had to trust God and surrender the day to Him.

Surrender happens when we let go of everything to lay hold of the most important thing.

Unlike the go-kart race, which was full of stress and strife, my willingness to surrender control on my wedding day allowed me to enjoy every minute of the day. When I raised my white flag, I stopped worrying about getting the outcome I wanted because I knew that God's will for us becoming husband and wife would be done either way. I knew I could trust Him to carry me through the day.

A fully surrendered heart is the antidote to fear and the gateway to freedom in the deep waters of life, because it's not focused on everything that's going wrong. Instead, it's focused on Jesus and everything He has done and made right.

Surrender happens when we let go of everything to lay hold of the most important thing. Although it might seem like a one-and-done action, it's actually a daily practice of making time to remember and rest in who God is and what He has done. It's a daily posture of choosing to trust God no matter the circumstance or outcome.

I shared the wedding story with you because when I look back on my life, I see that marrying Alex was the beginning of my exodus from bondage to freedom. As he and I sought to honor God with our marriage and love each other well, I experienced true, unconditional love that profoundly changed me.

Alex's love for me is a no-strings-attached, for-better-or-for-worse, I-love-you-no-matter-what, godly kind of love. I cannot even begin to count how many times in the first year of our marriage I messed up—but he still loved me. I would come home from work crying because of the pain my body was in, and he still loved me. I would regularly struggle to surrender my pain and heartache to God, but he loved me and helped me remember the truth.

Alex's love, along with the help I had received from my counselor, gave me a deeper glimpse of Jesus's love for me and the courage I needed to finally lay the broken pieces of my heart in God's hands and say, "Lord, here I am. Come and make me whole again. I trust you."

The secret to surrender is trust.

When we're afraid or struggling to keep our heads above water, we can keep striving in our own efforts or raise our white flag and trust God to take the broken pieces of our fractured hearts and love us back to wholeness in Him.

Every morning before I start the physical therapy and exercise regimen I have to do to keep my body from literally falling apart (yay, fragile

We can trust God to take the broken pieces of our fractured hearts and love us back to wholeness in Him.

connective tissue!), I lift up my hands to the heavens and tell my Savior, "God, help me trust You today. I surrender my life, health, circumstances —I surrender it all to You." Even when it hurts. Even when life is hard, yucky, and messy. In the good times and the bad times, I've learned that trusting God and surrendering my all to Him is the best way to live, because it takes the burden off my shoulders.

Beloved, He wants to take the burden from you today.

We were never meant to carry the weight of the world on our shoulders. Whatever the weight is, come and lay it down. Seek God, cultivate trust, and keep surrendering until it sticks.

GOING DEEPER

1. Does trusting others come easily, or is it difficult for you? What past experiences have made trust a more difficult or easier thing to do?
2. Do you trust God fully? If not, in what areas of your life do you struggle to trust Him fully, and why? What things are easier for you to trust Him with, and why?
3. How does the word *surrender* make you feel? In your mind, what does it look like to surrender your life fully to Christ?
4. How might your life change if you were to surrender every aspect of it daily to Christ?
5. What do you need to surrender today? Nail it to the cross, beloved. Lay it at His feet.

PRAYER

God, thank You for Your faithfulness. I cannot even begin to wrap my mind around everything You are and all You've done and are yet to do. It is beyond what I can comprehend. But Lord, even though some things are beyond my grasp, I ask for Your help as I go deeper into knowing more about You. Give me a hunger to know You. Help me trust You more and more with each passing day. If there is anything in me that I need to surrender, help me have the courage to do so today. Remind me of the freedom that is found in surrender and putting my faith in You. In Jesus's name. Amen.

PART TWO

Swimming with Jesus

CHAPTER FIVE

Faith Like the Ancients

*Now faith is confidence in what we hope for
and assurance about what we do not see.*

—*Hebrews 11:1*

J oining a sports team is a rite of passage in a person's life—at least I know it was for me. I remember the day I told my mom I wanted to join the swim team like it was yesterday. I burst through the door and handed her the flyer I'd received from the coach who had visited our fifth-grade classroom.

"Mommy, can I? Please, please, please? I want to be a swimmer!" I shouted as I danced up and down with a smile on my face.

"I don't know....Are you sure? You can barely make it across the pool without stopping," she reminded me.

But I'd already made up my mind. I believed I was destined to be a great swimmer. Even if the rest of the world told me otherwise, I was determined to succeed.

One of the things I loved about being on the swim team was the opportunity to be a part of something greater than myself. I could be having one of the worst days of my life, but none of that mattered during practices and meets. What mattered was that we were working together toward a common vision and goal.

We believed in each other, we believed in our team, and we believed that we would accomplish great things. But we also knew that accomplishing great things would require courage, training, and perseverance.

By the time I made it to high school, I was training around seventeen hours a week. And while many of my teammates had already peaked, I was well on my way to becoming one of the fastest swimmers in the area.

The training and competition were grueling, but with determination and grit, I persevered through my freshman year. My endurance was tested, however, when I began experiencing joint pain in my right shoulder and collarbone as a sophomore.

With each passing month, practices became more and more difficult, and my faith in myself as a swimmer was tested. My discouragement escalated over Christmas break when halfway into the main set my shoulder and collarbone issues flared up. *Maybe I can't finish this set. Maybe I won't break that school record after all*, I thought to myself. Then I looked up at the team banner hanging below the record board, which in big, bold letters read:

DREAM. BELIEVE. ACHIEVE.

Our coach loved these three words. So much so that he made them our team motto and ordered a banner with these words to display and encourage us during tough practices. Almost every day he reminded us that if we wanted to achieve great things and live a life worth living, we first had to believe.

And so, pain or no pain, I refused to give up on the dreams God had placed in my heart. No matter what roadblocks I encountered, I chose to keep believing; and when perseverance seemed impossible, I stayed the course. My swimming journey wasn't easy by any means, but some of the best moments of my life happened on that team, and I'm so glad I didn't give up. If I had thrown in the towel, I would have missed out on winning sectionals and competing with my team at the state championship finals.

Have you ever persevered through something you thought might be impossible to overcome? Have you ever struggled to believe in something? You wanted to persevere. You wanted to keep believing. But you couldn't. The opposition was too great, and you couldn't bear to be let down.

Because I know how hard it can be to persevere in sports and in life, I am deeply inspired by stories of people who endure despite debilitating circumstances. Whenever I start to feel like I'm drowning again, overcome by the cares and stresses of life, I turn to the Scriptures to read about the faith and perseverance of those who have gone before me. The stories of the ancients of faith give me hope and remind me that I, too, can have a faith like theirs as long as my heart is willing to believe. The same is true for you! Let's consider what they have to teach us.

What the Ancients Teach Us

It's easy to distance ourselves from the heroes of the Bible—the kings, queens, and battlefield warriors whose stories seem to resemble a Hollywood script but, in reality, are not much different from yours and mine. They entered the world just as we did: naked, unsure, and afraid. They suffered affliction. They endured hardships. They had doubts. They experienced triumph, heartache, and defeat.

As I flip through the pages of the Bible, the only difference I see between those marked by greatness and those not marked by greatness is a willingness to have faith. I think about Noah, Abraham, Moses, Joshua, Rahab, Esther, and King David, among the other ancient heroes who dwell within the pages of Scripture. These men and women were not remarkable because of who they were but because of what God was able to do through their faith.

As the youngest son of Jesse, David was the last one to be considered as a candidate for the next king of Israel when we meet him in 1 Samuel. While King Saul remained on the throne, God sent Samuel to David's hometown of Bethlehem to anoint the next king. One by one, Samuel examined seven of Jesse's eldest sons while David worked in the fields nearby. By the world's standards, any one of those sons was fit to be king, but God saw straight through their appearances to the condition of their hearts, letting Samuel know that He was not pleased.

> Samuel was blunt with Jesse, "GOD hasn't chosen any of these."
> Then he asked Jesse, "Is this it? Are there no more sons?"
> "Well, yes, there's the runt. But he's out tending the sheep."
> (1 Samuel 16:10-11 MSG)

Ouch. Talk about a hurtful and embarrassing description. I really feel for David here. The poor guy wasn't even there to introduce or defend himself, and he was already being labeled as the weakest link. Not the best first introduction, if you ask me.

Despite Jesse's reservations, he summoned for David to be brought before Samuel. My gut tells me, David knew something was up when he was called in from sheep-watching duty, but I'm sure he knew nothing about the gift he was about to receive. When Samuel laid eyes on David, God told him that this was the man He had sent him to meet in Bethlehem. This ordinary, small, humble, and unexpected shepherd was the man God wanted to be the next king of Israel.

I can only imagine David's surprise and bewilderment as Samuel commanded him to rise and receive the anointing. How unexplainable it must have felt to have the Spirit of God enter his being without warning, like a rush of wind reinvigorating him from the inside out (1 Samuel 16:13 MSG). Although David didn't know it at the time, he would become one of Israel's greatest kings. He would believe and trust that God was with him—even when his enemies threatened to destroy him or he stumbled into sin.

Throughout the Book of 2 Samuel, we see that by faith, David unified Israel and conquered the city of Jerusalem. By faith, David brought the Ark of the Covenant into Jerusalem. By faith, David established a powerful dynasty through which his offspring would be blessed. By faith, David laid the foundation for the Davidic line, the same line Jesus would descend from one day.

When we read about the accomplishments of David, it's easy to think he lived a life of luxury and splendor; but David's journey was not easy, and he was far from having it all together. If you've read the psalms written by David or the books of 1 and 2 Samuel, you know that the road God laid before him was full of twists, turns, trials, and tests. Even before he was king, David's faith was tested when God called him to face down a giant named Goliath.

As a champion fighter for the Philistine army, Goliath wasn't just your run-of-the-mill adversary. On top of some pretty impressive battlefield stats, the guy also registered about nine feet tall and who knows how many pounds. Now, I've never seen someone that tall, but if I did I'd probably run away in fear just like the rest of Goliath's opponents often did.

The Israelites and Philistines disagreed on a lot of things, but even in the midst of war they could agree on one thing: you don't want to mess with Goliath. David on the other hand saw things differently, and when the giant started challenging the Israelites to a duel, he wasn't afraid to stand up and fight. To the Israelite army, Goliath was a powerful giant;

but to David, this was simply a mortal man defying the armies of the living God.

David had an unshakable belief in the faithfulness of God. He knew that he would not be alone when he faced Goliath; God would fight with him and help him do the impossible by defeating a man who was twice his size.

I love David's response to Goliath's call for battle:

> "You come to me with sword, spear, and javelin, but I come to you in the name of the LORD of Heaven's Armies—the God of the armies of Israel, whom you have defied. Today the LORD will conquer you, and I will kill you and cut off your head. And then I will give the dead bodies of your men to the birds and wild animals, and the whole world will know that there is a God in Israel!" (1 Samuel 17:45-46 NLT)

Fighting Goliath posed a great danger to David, and the outcome was laced with uncertainty; yet David did not lose hope. Instead, he held on to his belief in God. It didn't matter what his peers thought or believed. In his heart, David chose to believe God would strengthen him to do the seemingly impossible. And later that day he did just that by defeating Goliath and turning away the entire Philistine army with just a sling and a stone.

None of this could have been accomplished by David's own strength. Try though he might, there's no way David ever could have mustered up enough faith on his own to accomplish all the good things he did in his seventy years of life.

There's no denying David wasn't perfect. In fact, he frequently gave in to sin. He had many wives, and he slept with another man's wife and arranged for that man to be murdered. He directly disobeyed God in taking a census of the people when God firmly told him not to. He fell short of God's glory just as you and I do. Yet despite all his flaws, David had this mark of greatness: deep faith in God. In Acts 13:22, God says that He found David to be "a man after my own heart." He had a deep desire to know and follow God.

This is what set David apart from the rest of the world, along with the other heroes of the Bible—many of whom are listed in Hebrews 11, known as the Hall of Faith. As this chapter so beautifully explains, these ordinary men and women are not remembered because of who they were. They are remembered for the legacy they left behind—a legacy of deep faith: being confident in what they hoped for and sure about what they did not see (Hebrews 11:1).

This is what the ancients were commended for. This is why we read their stories with wonder and awe, because their faith is the kind of faith we want. They weren't necessarily the coolest kids on the block or the people with the most money or the biggest palace. But their faith was strong, deep, wide, and rich; and that allowed them to achieve what others only dreamed of doing.

By faith, the earliest believers were able to understand that the universe was formed at God's command. By faith, Noah rescued his family from destruction by building a gigantic ark nearly one hundred years before the floodwaters even came. By faith, Abraham made his home in the promised land as a foreigner. By faith, Sarah gave birth to a son, even though she had been considered barren. By faith, Abraham offered Isaac as a sacrifice to God. By faith, Moses regarded disgrace for the sake of God as of greater value than the treasures of Egypt. By faith, Moses left Egypt, not fearing Pharaoh's anger; he persevered because he believed God was with him. By faith, the walls of Jericho fell, after the army marched around them for seven days. By faith, Esther risked her life to save an entire nation.

The most notable moments of recorded biblical history would not have happened without faith. The ancients teach us that faith is necessary in order to know God and live for Him. I don't know about you, but I don't want a faith that looks like so many others in this world—half-hearted and timid. I want a bold, overcoming faith like the ancients. Let's consider how our biblical ancestors demonstrated and exercised courageous faith.

The Ancients Accepted the Gift of Faith

The first step in living out our faith is to turn to God and receive the gift of faith He wants to multiply in us. I wrote briefly in the last chapter about one of the happiest days of my life: my wedding day. Between the outdoor photo shoot, an emotional ceremony, dancing with friends and family, and eating copious amounts of steak, asparagus, and cupcakes, it was a picture-perfect day full of great joy and love. Looking back, I can honestly say I wouldn't change a thing—except maybe the amount of sleep I got the night before.

With an early flight to catch the day after the wedding, Alex and I didn't open presents until after the honeymoon, which made for an even more exciting homecoming. As expected, most of the gifts were items from the registry, but toward the end of our opening spree we discovered a sleek envelope hidden underneath one of the boxes. Inside was a check with an unbelievable amount of zeroes.

"Oh, gracious," I said, my voice trembling with unbelief. "We can't accept this."

I knew the check came with great sacrifice for the person who wrote it, and that made it incredibly difficult for me to accept the gift. After all, I'd already had a beautiful wedding and honeymoon. This was too much. Too good to be true. I didn't deserve this.

"Maybe they put an extra zero by mistake or something," I told Alex. "Do you think we should double check?"

"Sweetie, I don't think someone would accidentally write a check like this," he replied. "C'mon. You should be excited about this. This is amazing!"

Amazing or not, the gift still seemed too good to be true until we deposited it at the bank the next day.

That's how faith can seem to a lot of us. As sons and daughters of a ridiculously generous God, sometimes it's hard to wrap our minds around or accept the gift of faith. We've been told what faith produces in our lives—obedience, perseverance, hope, and salvation—but in our brokenness, part of us may feel that it's just too good to be true.

Beloved, please know I say this in love because I've been there: If you think the gift of faith is too good to be true, you have been deceived. Our God is a good God, and every good and perfect gift is from Him. You are not destined for misery. You are destined for good things! Things He planned for you long, long ago (Ephesians 2:10).

I know what you're thinking: Certainly, having courageous faith can't be as easy as just turning to God. There has to be more work on our part, right? Wrong. This is the beauty and simplicity of the gospel: "It is by grace you have been saved, through faith—and this is not from yourselves, it is the gift of God—not by works, so that no one can boast" (Ephesians 2:8-9). We exercise faith when we look to Jesus and His work on the cross, which brings us salvation—receiving it as a gift. For the ancients who lived before the cross, they looked ahead in faith to the coming Messiah, Jesus Christ, just as we look back to His death and resurrection. And as those living on

> Deep faith and relationship with our Father is a gift. When we say yes to Him, He spurs us on to keep believing.

this side of the cross, we also receive the gift of the Holy Spirit when we choose to accept the gift of faith and believe in Christ.

Faith in the Greek is *pistis*,[1] and the root of pistis is *peithô*, meaning "to persuade or be persuaded" or "yield to."[2] When we yield our hearts in an act of faith, God takes that yielding and multiplies our faith so that we can know Him and enter into relationship with Him. Deep faith and relationship with our Father is a gift. When we say yes to Him, He spurs us on to keep believing. Our choice, then, is whether or not we will yield and receive faith in the first place.

Thousands of years later, our definition of faith looks nothing like its origin. Today faith often is associated with our own efforts. Our culture has made faith out to be something that is considered too much work and unnecessary. But faith isn't meant to create more work in our lives; it is a gift that is meant to usher us into a beautiful way of living.

To some, faith might seem like some ancient, elusive, and exclusive thing, but it's not. The same gift of faith that the ancients possessed is available to every single human being. What is the difference between the faithful ancients and many of us today? They accepted the gift. People like Abraham, Sarah, Jacob, Moses, and Rahab welcomed faith into their lives even if it didn't always make sense. They exercised faith and trust in God even when it looked foolish to others.

We don't have to do anything to earn this gift. It's free for the taking, and every single day we have the choice to pick it up. All we have to do is take the first step and say, "Lord, I believe." Then each day we can ask Him to help us take up the shield of faith as His Word commands in Ephesians 6:16 (more on that in chapter 7). And as we've seen, even in our doubt we can ask Him to help us overcome our unbelief (Mark 9:24).

The Ancients Modeled Devotion

The ancients also demonstrated faith through their ongoing devotion to God.

Though we live on the side of history where we can freely access God and the Holy Spirit without barriers because of Jesus's work on the cross, many of us who believe in Him are not making room for God to move in our lives. We're content with a more convenient faith, as if our relationship with God is like our relationship with fast food.

I'll have a blessed life with a side of fries, please.

We may laugh, but if we take a step back and examine our hearts, can we say that our level of devotion is anything like those in the Hebrews 11 Hall of Faith? Honestly, for the majority of Christians in the West today, I don't think it is.

For many of us, faith equates to going to church on Sundays, praying before meals and bedtime, and being kind and loving to others—if it's convenient for us. We're generally too stressed, distracted, and busy for God. In a world where so much seems to be going wrong, we often doubt His goodness. And in our busyness, we either don't have time or make time to read our Bibles and seek God's face.

A part of us may long for a deeper faith, but so often this desire is drowned out by never-ending to-do lists and addictive technologies. When life gets messy and the mountain of faith seems insurmountable, we tend to view faith as some ancient fairy tale. We hear stories about faith that can move mountains, but that kind of faith seems too good to be true and out of our reach. And so, many of us settle for a convenient, surface-level faith—or no faith at all. The problem with this approach to life is that at the end of the day, when everything is stripped away and we're left standing alone in the valley of our circumstances, faith is the only thing we really have to hold on to. We need faith if we are going to survive this life, and that means we simply cannot afford to lose it or settle for something less than what God wants to give us.

If there's anything God and the ancients have taught me about faith, it's that a convenient faith never satisfies. Like a cheap fast-food burger, it seems appealing enough but does not fill us up. Our souls are left wanting something better—something more. Whether we realize it or not, we need ongoing devotion to God.

Waking up early every morning to delight in God's presence and meditate on His Word is not convenient, but it's priceless.

Remember that first counseling appointment I had? I went home craving to read the Bible; but if I'm being honest, I wasn't exactly yearning for God at that point—I was yearning for Him to fix my problems. But true to His loving, gracious nature, God didn't take my problems away. Instead He met me in my mess and began to change and move in my heart. And the more He moved in my heart and helped me find joy in my circumstances, the more in love with Him I became.

Today as God continues to work in my life, I can say with confidence that I don't want the healing without the healer. I don't crave God to simply fix my problems so I can go on my merry way. I crave God's presence in my problems so I can experience the deep joy, peace, and satisfaction that supersedes anything this world could ever offer.

Sure, waking up early every morning to delight in God's presence and meditate on His Word is not convenient, but it's priceless.

Psalm 119 is a passage of Scripture I frequently turn to when I notice convenience creeping into my faith life. It's an incredibly convicting chapter of the Bible, but it's also an encouraging model of the life and thoughts of a devoted believer. The psalmist implores us to choose the way of faithfulness by setting our hearts on God's laws (v. 30), seeking God with devotion, and delighting in His Word, which sustains and preserves our life (v. 50). As life has brought new challenges and trials, these verses have become something I pray daily:

Your hands made me and formed me;
give me understanding to learn your
commands.
May those who fear you rejoice when they
see me,
for I have put my hope in your word.
I know, LORD, that your laws are righteous,
and that in faithfulness you have
afflicted me.
May your unfailing love be my comfort,
according to your promise to your
servant.
Let your compassion come to me that I
may live,
for your law is my delight.
May the arrogant be put to shame for
wronging me without cause;
but I will meditate on your precepts.
May those who fear you turn to me,
those who understand your statutes.
May I wholeheartedly follow your decrees,
that I may not be put to shame.

(Psalm 119:73-80)

May we all follow wholeheartedly after Jesus, where our faith will never be put to shame. This is what it means to demonstrate faith through ongoing devotion.

The Ancients Dared to Believe

Besides receiving the gift of faith and demonstrating ongoing devotion, the ancients dared to believe God—even when they were afraid.

No one thought our high school girls' swim team was capable of breaking a long-standing record, let alone winning sectional finals. We were the underdogs, the team who always got second place, the ones who dreamed big but somehow missed the mark at the championships every year. But not this year. Not my senior year. Not on my watch.

Our coach had crunched the stats, and according to his predictions we actually had a shot this time. He believed in us, and that belief helped us step up to the challenge in faith. This was our time; this was our chance; and we weren't going down without a fight.

As cocaptain of the team, I gave a short pump-up talk before sectionals began; and with every word I spoke, I felt my faith increase. The more I talked about winning, the more I saw my teammates' faith increasing too. By the end of my talk, most of the girls were nodding their heads in agreement. Sure, there was still a little bit of uncertainty in each of our hearts. We knew the odds were stacked against us. But for the first time in a long time, our team deeply believed we could win; and that made all the difference.

It's amazing what can happen when we allow faith to rise within us—when we consider for the first time that the extraordinary, seemingly impossible thing is actually within our reach. Even the tiniest seed of faith can give birth to hope if we give it the space it needs to grow in our hearts.

Just as our coach had predicted, the meet was close right up to the very last event: the 400-freestyle relay, which I happened to be leading. My adrenaline soared as I stared at the heat sheet, thinking about everything that was at stake.

We've got this. We're going to win. This is our time. Like a song on repeat, these are the truths I claimed in the minutes leading up to the big race.

To my relief, Coach called us over to say a few words just before our relay team went to line up behind the blocks.

"Girls, gather 'round and listen close," he said. "OK, you've trained hard all year. Now this is our chance. You see that banner up there? Dream, believe, achieve? You've dreamed. You've believed. Now it's time to achieve."

And with that, we walked over to huddle behind the blocks before the race. Like I said, no one expected us to win. One of the swimmers on the relay was swimming injured, and another had been swapped out in a last-minute strategy change. We had a lot to be uncertain and afraid of, but in the unity of the huddle, we decided none of that mattered. We were going to win this thing. And with a little bit of faith and a whole lot of hope, that's exactly what we did.

We didn't win because we were necessarily the fastest, strongest swimmers. We won because we dared to believe. We dared to let faith rise. We dared to hope in spite of our fears and hesitations.

Beloved, what might happen if we allowed hope to rise in our hearts today? What if we dared to put our faith back where it belongs and believe God for our lives, despite all the fears and hesitations we have? What if we made practicing faith a habit and living from a place of trust our only way of living?

This is how we get back to our faith roots: we dare to believe. Like Abraham, we dare to believe that God's ways are for our good. Like Sarah, we dare to believe that nothing is impossible with God. Like Moses, we dare to believe in the power of the unseen. Like Joshua, we dare to believe that God will help us be strong and courageous because He is in control. Like David, we dare to believe that God is with us no matter what. Like Esther, we dare to believe that God created us for a specific purpose.

For me, daring to believe is daring to trust that God is able to heal me—and even if He doesn't, I'm going to be OK. What is one thing God is daring you to believe Him for today?

The Ancients Practiced Faith

Another way the ancients demonstrated their faith was simply to *practice* it. The beautiful thing is that if faith is something we *practice*, then this means it doesn't have to be perfect. Aren't you relieved to know that we don't have to get this faith thing right 100 percent of the time?

I like to think about practicing faith the same way I think about maintaining a healthy lifestyle. Some days I'm a healthy-living champ. I'm active every few hours; I make wise decisions for breakfast, lunch, and dinner; I take brain breaks; I vow to not let anxiety get the best of me; I get in bed at the appropriate hour. Then there are the days I fail. I don't get up and move throughout the day; I forget to plan meals in advance; I power through the workday for the sake of efficiency; I let my emotions get the best of me and become an anxious mess; I fall asleep way later than I had planned. But whenever I fail, I pick myself up and start again.

In my walk with Jesus over the years, practicing faith has looked a lot like trying to live a healthy lifestyle. Some days my faith is strong. I'm in the Word; I pray throughout the day; I sing songs of praise; I lay my burdens at God's feet; I trust Him with everything, especially the things that are completely out of my control. Other days my faith is weak. I get swept away by the waves of life; I don't claim God's promises over my situation; I forget to pray; I sin; I don't know if I can fully trust God. But just as I start again with healthy habits, I start again with the practices of a mustard seed faith—of simply reaching out and beginning again.

"To practice" means to perform an activity or exercise a skill repeatedly or regularly in order to improve or maintain one's proficiency.[3] God knows that we won't always get things right as we practice faith. Some days we will do well and win the fight for faith; other days we will fall behind or lose. What's important is not that we "out believe" everyone else but that we simply keep on practicing faith. We dare to believe and see what God might do as a result of that belief.

The world tells us that faith isn't worth the fight...

It's too much work.
It's a dying practice.
It can't really make a difference.
It's a silly, ancient thing.

Here's the thing: The enemy of our souls rules this world (1 John 5:19) and wants to outsmart us with evil schemes (2 Corinthians 2:11). He wants you and me to be hopeless and confused. He doesn't want us to open our hearts to the possibility of faith and trust anyone or anything, especially God. Instead, he wants us to be vulnerable to his schemes, and we are; because over time, as the world has continued to give us reasons not to practice faith, we have bought into the lie that perhaps nothing is worth our complete trust. As a result, we've become increasingly hopeless.

As we practice faith, living by faith becomes easier with each passing day.

But the same words Jesus spoke over His disciples are true for us today: "Blessed are those who have not seen and yet have believed" (John 20:29).

God's Word is clear: faith is more precious than gold (1 Peter 1:7). It's the most valuable and precious thing we could ever hope to possess. And it's not too much work or out of date. It's a beautiful, priceless gift—the mark of greatness and victory. And practicing faith makes all the difference in our lives, just as it did for David and the other ancients of the faith. We don't have to get it right every time; we just have to keep practicing it. And as we *practice* faith, *living* by faith becomes easier with each passing day.

The Ancients Possessed the Three Ps of a Deep Faith

We know that we can trust God and that faith in Him is the only thing that can save us. So with the right perspective, we can develop a faith like the ancients by remembering what I call the three Ps of a deep faith: rest in His promises, ask for provision, and resolve to persevere. I rely on the three Ps almost every day to just keep swimming by faith. Let's consider each one.

1. Rest in His Promises

Faith starts with choosing to believe and trust God, but it doesn't stop there. Once we reach out to God in faith and surrender our lives to Him, we have to bathe ourselves in His promises as the ancients of faith did. Just as we bathe our bodies to keep ourselves healthy, so must we bathe our minds with God's promises to keep our souls healthy.

The Bible is full of hundreds of promises, but here are the top ten promises that have helped me most in my faith journey, both after my first faith crisis and in the many battles I've faced since then. If your faith needs to be strengthened today, take courage in knowing these promises are just as true for you as they are for me. God's promises are not exclusive to certain people or groups; they are true for all of us!

1. God promises to never leave us or forsake us. (Deuteronomy 31:6)
2. God promises to take our despair and doubt and give us a new heart and spirit of courage and faith. (Ezekiel 36:26)
3. God promises protection from harm or danger. (Psalm 91:4-6)
4. God promises to supply our every need. (Philippians 4:19)
5. God promises to give us wisdom and guide us. (Psalm 32:8; Isaiah 30:21)
6. God promises to give us peace. (Isaiah 26:3; Psalm 119:165)

7. God promises the enemy will flee when we draw near to Him. (James 4:7-10)

8. God promises deliverance from fear when we seek Him. (Psalm 34:4)

9. God promises to work all things together for our good. (Romans 8:28)

10. God promises victory through Jesus Christ. (Romans 8:37)

When we remember God's promises, our hearts are strengthened, renewed, and refreshed so that we can keep our eyes above the waves and fixed on Jesus in faith. When we learn to trade our problems for the promises of our Creator, we can handle the unknown swells because our hearts have been steadied by what we know.

One of these promises, *God promises to supply our every need*, leads us to the next piece of the three-P puzzle.

2. Ask for Provision

Remembering God's provision is one of the most important things we can do for our faith. Here's why: When our faith is shaken and we're in a high-sea battle, it's extremely comforting to know that our needs are going to be taken care of. Fear might rear its ugly head for a moment, and we might not have a clue how we are going to make it to the other side of the trial, but when we trust God to meet our needs no matter what, that changes everything.

Looking back on my first faith crisis, I can see God's provision in directing me to the counselor's office, giving me an amazing man to call husband, and providing me with family and friends who fiercely supported me. But His provision didn't stop there. No, our God is a God who never ceases to provide for His children, and I'd like to share with you another story that happened recently to further illustrate this point.

One month after Alex and I bought his business and moved halfway across the country, I lost my job in a round of company layoffs. The company I'd been with for several years had allowed me to work long-distance for a short time, but now they needed to make some cutbacks. So, as a remote employee, I was one of the first to be placed on the chopping block. Had the layoff happened at any other point in our marriage, we would have had nothing to worry about. But at this time our finances were stretched and our faith was shaken. In the span of a few months, we were earning less than a third of what we had made before our move—barely enough to get by. Now what would happen to us?

"We wish you all the best, Lauren," the human resources manager had said.

"Thanks, and God bless you," I replied, trying to hold back my tears until I hung up. When the call was over, I lay on the ground and stared at the ceiling until the tears started to run. And that's when I heard a still, small voice.

Beloved, I am with you. I have already gone before you. I'm going to take care of this and carry you from here, just like I've carried you in every other hard season of life.

As I allowed the peace and love of the Holy Spirit to flood my heart, I could feel my faith being strengthened. I recalled the words of Philippians 4:19: "And my God will meet all your needs according to the riches of his glory in Christ Jesus," and I breathed deeply, reminding myself that because of my great God, everything would be OK.

God has promised provision for every torrent and trial.

That medical bill you don't know how you are going to pay; that to-do list that you feel like you don't have time for; that depressive episode you don't know if you're going to make it out of alive—God promises to meet every single need along the way. If we know this to be true, then in faith we can turn to God and praise Him as we await the provision. We can live expectantly with great hope as we recall all the ways in which God has provided for our needs in the past.

The same God who met your needs and rescued you from sinking yesterday, last year, or many years ago is the same God who will continue to meet your needs today and for the rest of eternity. Although we don't always know what God's provision is going to look like, we can trust Him to fill us with His living water and give us our daily bread when we turn to Him.

See how Scripture describes God's continual provision after He delivered the Israelites from slavery and the hand of Pharaoh's army:

> Then Moses cried out to the LORD, and the LORD showed him a piece of wood. He threw it into the water, and the water became fit to drink.
> (Exodus 15:25)

> Then the LORD said to Moses, "I will rain down bread from heaven for you...."
> "I have heard the grumbling of the Israelites. Tell them, 'At twilight you will eat meat, and in the morning you will be filled with bread. Then you will know that I am the LORD your God.'"
> (Exodus 16:4, 12)

Did you catch what happened before God made the water fit to drink? Prayer preceded God's provision. Moses cried out to God about a real need, and God was faithful to meet that need. Hallelujah! Thank you, Jesus! Amen! And He will do the same for us when we cry out to Him in prayer, asking Him to make up for where we are lacking.

The day after I lost my job, I had a brief emotional setback and watched a lot of chick flicks, stayed in my pajamas all day, ate soup out of the can, and demolished enough chocolate chip cookies to feed an army. I grumbled all kinds of "this is not fair" clichés to God. But when I climbed into bed that night, my heart was heavy and sick. I knew I needed to shore up my faith, move on with my life, and trust that God had a plan in all this. So, come dawn the next day, I decided I was done complaining. I didn't want to be like the Israelites, who failed to remember God's track record of faithfulness. Instead, I had a new game plan: strap on my tennis shoes and prayer walk around my neighborhood until my feet failed me.

I would pray, "God, I don't know how you're going to provide, but I need you to show up in this. God, my hands are completely open wide. My life is fully surrendered to you. Remember your servant and meet our needs, Lord Jesus."

In this season of transition and change, God sent several freelance design and marketing projects my way to help Alex and me make ends meet. Then, after praying fervently for months, more steady provision came through—just at the right time.

I hope my story helps you remember a time when the Lord provided in a supernatural way for you, a family member, or a friend. Hang on to those stories, beloved, and don't be afraid to ask God to help meet your need when one arises. He longs to be gracious to you (Isaiah 30:18).

3. Resolve to Persevere

Finally, we must resolve to persevere. My dad's side of the family, the Hardys, have a saying: "Hardys never quit." As a child I was raised to stay the course, live tenaciously, and never give up. When I look at my bloodline, there's no denying these traits are what set our family apart. For us, the term *hardy* goes beyond just having a strong last name. It's a mindset—a way of life that has enabled us to overcome and keep the faith. Though I changed my last name when Alex and I married, these persistent attributes remain strong in me. In the words of my father, "You can take the Hardy out of the name, but you can't take the Hardy out of the girl."

In the same way, we have a biblical bloodline that helps us persevere when our faith is tested. You see, you and I belong to the family of Jesus, the most perseverant person to walk this earth. He persevered to death on a cross in order to accomplish God's will and set us free, and we too can persevere in faith when we remember all Christ suffered and endured on our behalf.

You Have More Faith Than You Think

Last year, I made a new friend while traveling to a writer's conference with one of my ministry partners, Heather. Though we'd only just met her, we felt compelled to ask this woman to join us for dinner at a Thai restaurant nearby. As the summer rolls, pineapple fried rice, and pad woon sen arrived at our table, we talked about the different passions and callings God has placed on our lives.

For Heather and me, it's encouraging women to experience deep courage, faith, and joy in life. For this woman, it's encouraging women to seek God's kingdom in the mundane.

"I'm so excited about your book on faith!" my new friend told me. "I don't know if you have room for it in the book, but there's an illustration I'd love to share with you if you have time."

I leaned in to listen as she shared this nugget of wisdom with me, and I knew that one of the reasons God had brought us together was so that her words could have a place in this book.

"A lot of people read the Bible and are intimidated by the faith of those who have gone before us," she said. "We think we can't experience the same kind of faith. But here's what someone told me once that wrecked me. They said, 'We have more faith than we think. Every day, we turn on our coffee machine and trust it to give us the liquid fuel we need to get through the day. We back out of our driveways and trust our cars to safely get us from point A to point B. We trust our loved ones to be there for us no matter what. It's not a question of do we have faith; it's a question of do we have faith in God?"

Her words reverberated in my mind during the entire car ride home, and to this day I cannot shake the illustration because it's true. Beloved, faith is possible for every single one of us, and we have a greater capacity for it than we might think. This is the truth I hope you will take to heart and start applying in your relationship with Jesus. And as you keep saying yes to Him, He will increase your faith in ways that exceed anything you could ever imagine.

GOING DEEPER

1. Which biblical hero's story of faith inspires you the most, and why?

2. In what ways has convenience crept into your relationship with Jesus? How can you take that awareness and use it to go deeper with Him?

3. Which of the three Ps is hardest for you to remember and practice? Which is easiest? What can you do to remember and practice the three Ps on a regular basis?

4. Can you remember a time when the Lord provided in a supernatural way for you, a family member, or a friend? How did God come through when, from a worldly standpoint, all hope seemed lost?

PRAYER

Jesus, thank You for Your promises. I know that I can count on Your Word. Let faith arise in me today. Lord, I ask You to provide my every need as I journey deeper with You. Help me to persevere. Give me a heart that refuses to back down against the waves and the schemes of the enemy. Give me a heart that believes You with every fiber of my being. I want a faith like the ancients. When my time has come, I want to hear You say, "Well done, my good and faithful servant" (Matthew 25:21 NLT). In Jesus's name. Amen.

CHAPTER SIX

Pursuing God

*Let the seeking man reach a place where life and lips join to
say continually, "Be thou exalted," and a thousand
minor problems will be solved at once.*

—A. W. Tozer[1]

W hen the waves of anxiety came crashing over me in high school,
I read a lot of books and listened to a lot of music. In the early
stages of my faith journey, this is how I pursued God. I desperately longed
for more of Him, and books and songs were the only ways I knew how to
communicate with Him at the time.

On the weekends, I'd grab my iPod and pound the pavement around
our neighborhood while blaring Starfield's "Rediscover You" on repeat. I
sang along in my head as the band played the song, desperately wanting
God to help me and give me a sign that He was listening. But no number
of repeats brought me closer to the One I was trying to pursue. And so by

the time I took off my running shoes, I had already forgotten and given up on hearing from God.

Have you ever experienced this in your faith journey? You tried pursuing God in faith but gave up because you didn't seem to hear from Him right away? Me too. Been there, done that.

As people of faith, we are called to seek God above all else (Matthew 6:33). We are told that when we seek Him with all our heart and all our soul, we will find Him (Deuteronomy 4:29). But what happens when we're drowning and don't know where to reach? What happens when we have the faith of a mustard seed but don't feel Him near? What does it mean if God is silent and we feel lost in our pursuit? And how should we respond? These are the questions we will explore in this chapter.

God Is Always with Us

I'm always intrigued to learn what someone's last words were, because they can reveal a lot about a person's character and how they lived life. Here are a few of my favorites: Blues singer Bessie Smith died saying, "I'm going, but I'm going in the name of the Lord." Italian artist Raphael's last word was simply "Happy." When William Henry Seward, architect of the Alaska Purchase, was asked if he had any final words, all he had to say was, "Nothing, only 'love one another.'"[2] And though I don't know the time or place Jesus will call me home, I can imagine my last words will be something along the lines of "You are my joy, Jesus. Take me home!"

If Jesus promises to always be with us, we can trust and believe He's here even when we can't feel Him.

Our last words can hold deep significance, and when shared or recorded, they have the power to leave an eternal impact. The same principles applied to our Savior's last words. Before Jesus breathed His last on the cross, He said, "It is finished" (John 19:30). But do you remember what the resurrected Jesus said before he ascended into heaven and took His place at the right hand of God? These were the last words He chose to share with His disciples: "And surely I am with you always, to the very end of the age" (Matthew 28:20).

Of all the things Jesus could have said to His disciples and to future Christ followers like you and me, He used His last moments to remind us that He is always with us. Not sometimes. Not only when He feels like it. *Always*. This was the last promise our beloved Savior chose to give us before He left earth to join the Father in heaven.

Can we pause for a second and reflect on how precious and beautiful this promise is?

If Jesus promises to always be with us, we can trust and believe He's here even when we can't feel Him. And if Jesus is always in our midst, then we can be encouraged to keep pursuing Him until we experience His manifest presence in our own lives. In the words of A. W. Tozer,

> God is here when we are wholly unaware of it. He is *manifest* only when and as we are aware of His presence. On our part there must be surrender to the Spirit of God, for His work it is to show us the Father and the Son. If we cooperate with Him in loving obedience, God will manifest Himself to us, and that manifestation will be the difference between a nominal Christian life and a life radiant with the light of His face.[3]

I don't like it when God feels distant, but over time I've learned that when silence creeps into my spiritual life, the disconnect is usually because of something happening on my end. Maybe I felt like I couldn't trust Him, and so I chose not to and took matters into my own hands. Maybe I didn't actually surrender the situation to God. Maybe I failed to be obedient to something God told me to do. Or maybe I was simply struggling through grief or disappointment. Let me encourage you, friend. Whatever disconnect you're experiencing with God, it won't last forever. Actually, your breath is evidence that you *are* connected, because God is the Source of our breath and His very Spirit dwells within us. In time you will *feel* connected again. And sometimes all it takes is a willingness to trust, surrender, or obey.

To echo Tozer's point, our response to silence should be to keep believing and pursuing connection with Him. We do not relent until the walls separating us from our Father have come down. We keep praying and meditating on God's Word until we experience Him again and the answer becomes clear. Courageous faith is believing God is with us even if our feelings persuade us to believe otherwise, because our feelings are not the boss of us.

This theme of pursuing relationship with God is persistent throughout Scripture, and in this chapter we're going to look more specifically at how to do that in our own lives. Faith is born when we first believe, but it deepens when we learn to passionately pursue connection with the One we put our faith in. And there are some practical ways we can pursue relationship with our always-present God through everyday routines, choices, and practices.

Routines: A Tale of Two Mornings

Mornings are built on routines. After we wake up, we do things such as take the dog out or take care of the kids, make breakfast, shower, get dressed, and head to the gym, work, or whatever our daily routine might be. Without routines, most of us would be unorganized, late, or just downright unproductive. But sometimes a routine can become destructive to our spiritual lives, and good things designed to make our life better can become idols. Let me explain by sharing a tale of two mornings.

Morning #1

While most of the world is sound asleep, I wake up before my alarm rings and immediately grab my phone. After rubbing my tired eyes open, I refresh my email and social networks feeds to see what I missed while I was sleeping. Then I slip into my swimsuit, grab my keys, and head for the pool.

Aside from eating breakfast, swimming is the morning activity I cherish most. But when I pull up to the facility, I receive an email alerting me that the pool is closed.

"You've got to be kidding me!" I shout to an empty car, frustrated and angered by the inconvenience of not being able to do what I enjoy.

At least there's still breakfast, I think to myself.

I compromise for an elliptical workout and speed home to whip up my usual breakfast: chocolate-peanut-butter-banana oatmeal. My husband says it looks like motor fuel, but to me it's liquid gold. Give me a bowl of chocolate oatmeal and coffee, and I'm in breakfast paradise. When it's time to take the pot off the stove, I wait for the food to cool and shovel every last bite into my mouth as quickly as I can without even saying grace. But by the time I'm finished, I'm not satisfied. I only wish there was more.

I look at the clock and realize I'm already fifteen minutes behind schedule, so I hurry upstairs to dive into work before losing more precious time. Before I know it, it's dinnertime and I haven't even given one thought to God.

Morning #2

I wake up with joy to the dawn of a new day. Who needs an alarm when you have the sun to wake you up? I fight the urge to grab my phone and instead pause to pray and thank God for new mercies and a fresh start:

This day is yours, Lord. Do what You want to do in me today. I surrender this day and myself to You. Thank You for dwelling in my heart. May I feel and sense Your presence all around me today. I know You are active and always at work. Help me see You in all things—both big and small. In Jesus's name. Amen.

I open my Bible app and try to commit the verse of the day to memory. As I brush my teeth and put on my swimsuit, I thank God for another chance to swim.

When I arrive at the pool, all of the lanes are occupied, but I don't get frustrated or angry. Instead, I strike up a conversation with one of the seniors who has stopped swimming and is taking a break at the wall.

"You want to swim with me?" she asks.

"Are you sure?" I reply.

"Of course!"

With my cap and goggles firmly secured around my head, I push off the wall and continue my conversation with God. The more I talk to Him, the more joy floods my heart. On my way home, I sing a few of my favorite praise songs and roll my windows down to feel the wind on my face. I don't care that it's only forty-five degrees outside. I want to breathe in the cool, crisp, and fresh air. I want to smell those sweet Carolina pines.

As I prepare for breakfast, I thank God for the wonderful food He has given me access to, and I ask Him to bless those who are not as fortunate as I. When the oatmeal is ready to eat, I savor every bite as I remind myself that God is the only One who can truly satisfy.

I look at the clock and decide to spend another five minutes with God—this time in His Word. Then I continue my day, doing the things I have planned to do. Before I know it, it's dinnertime and I've seen and felt God in more ways than one.

Pursuing God starts in the morning. When we wake up we have two options: we can lay down our idols and seek satisfaction in God, or we can push Him aside as we look to earthly things to take care of our wants and needs.

When I say idol, I'm not talking about ancient figurines and statues; I'm talking about anything that takes the place God should have in our hearts. When I think about the idols I turn to for satisfaction in the morning, three objects come to mind: my phone, exercise, and food. I like being connected to the world. I like jump-starting my day by working out. And I really like breakfast. But none of those things were designed to satisfy my soul the way that pursuing relationship with God can.

Ongoing connection is key to experiencing deep satisfaction and relationship with Christ.

I love the way Beth Moore puts it in her Bible study *Breaking Free*:

> Our wise and merciful Lord creates every one of us with a God-shaped void in our lives so we will seek Him. Dissatisfaction is not a terrible thing. It's a God-thing. The terrible thing is when we don't let it lead us to Christ. He wants us to find the only thing that will truly satiate our thirsty and hungry hearts.[4]

Whether we work from home, commute, or are a night-shift rock star, we all have been given the opportunity to pursue God in our daily routines. For me, that means setting aside time to pray and read the Bible in the morning and go on a prayer walk or two during the day. But maybe your schedule doesn't allow for long periods of focused time in prayer and God's Word. That's OK. The goal isn't to see how many moments of quiet time you can squeeze into one day. The goal is that no matter what our routines look like, we choose to focus our thoughts on God from the moment we wake up to the moment we go to sleep. Ongoing connection is key to experiencing deep satisfaction and relationship with Christ.

Following Jesus's Example

Fullness is found in relationship with Christ and Christ alone (Ephesians 3:19). So when we find ourselves dissatisfied or our faith shaken, we can know that whatever is broken within us—whatever damage has been done by the waves that are breaking over us—will be made whole when we pursue God above all else, no matter what. In His presence there is fullness of joy (Psalm 16:11), and thanks to the saving work of Jesus, His presence surrounds us always—even now as you're reading this book.

No greater story illustrates how to pursue connection with God than the story of Jesus praying in the Garden of Gethsemane before He was betrayed and arrested. I can only imagine the size of the waves that were surrounding Jesus in this moment. When I read about the hours and days leading up to His death, I picture the waves raging way above His head, threatening to pull Him under. He knew what was coming. He knew it wasn't going to be pretty. But He didn't run away or sink into despair. He reached out to God and, with great faith and courage, held on to hope.

After studying Jesus's actions in the Garden of Gethsemane and as He was dying on the cross, I have identified five behaviors or choices that set Jesus's pursuit of God apart from our often feeble and conditional efforts. We can follow Jesus's example to keep ourselves from drifting away from God and keep our hearts hungry for more of God.

1. Jesus was all in.

Before Jesus was betrayed, denied, arrested, beaten, mocked, and condemned to death on a cross, He went to the Garden of Gethsemane. The accounts of what happened in the garden are recorded in three out of the four Gospels in the New Testament—Matthew, Mark, and Luke—and each account reveals another layer of the story.

Here's what really messes me up. Because Jesus was both the Son of God and a man, He knew what was coming. He knew every prophecy His Father had foretold about Him—and that His job was to fulfill each one.

Jesus knew He was destined to die. In the Gospel of Mark, He predicts His death three times.

Let's just stop right there for a moment. I don't know about you, but if I knew I was destined to die, I'd probably stop working, buy a one-way ticket to the Caribbean, and give the rest of my money away. But Jesus didn't cash it all in so He could spend His last days in comfort. Instead, He stayed true to His mission to set the captives free and conquer the grave (Isaiah 61:1; Isaiah 25:7-8). Part of staying true to the mission also meant staying intimately connected to the Father—the source of all strength—which is why we see Jesus praying and pursuing God on numerous accounts throughout the Gospels.

As followers of Jesus, we too have been given a mission. Our lives have divine purpose. While we don't always know every detail of our mission, we can choose to seek God from beginning to end just as Jesus did.

Jesus did not tiptoe into faith—into trusting His Father's plans. He dove headfirst, joyfully, into deep faith. He was all in, all the time. The question is, are we?

It's important to remember that while we can strive to be like Jesus, we will never reach His perfection in this lifetime. In reality, we are constantly being transformed into His image with ever-increasing glory (2 Corinthians 3:18). Keeping this in mind, we can breathe a little easier knowing all-in faith doesn't mean we won't have doubts or get distracted from time to time. We're not Jesus. We're human, and we make mistakes. Instead, all-in faith means forging forward in the face of adversity and choosing the righteous road over the facile freeway.

2. Jesus put self on a shelf.

Remember the tale of two mornings from earlier in this chapter? Both are true experiences I've lived. I know the picture I painted of myself in Morning #1 isn't pretty, because it's self-focused; but when I find myself struggling with selfishness, sadly it's an accurate picture. I'm not as apt to make time for God when I'm feeding my selfish tendencies. As God continues to work in my life, I'm thankful to say the vast majority of my mornings look more like Morning #2 these days. But when I see a #1 scenario start to take shape, I remind myself to put my "self on a shelf," because that's exactly what Jesus did. In the garden and on the cross, Jesus could have rewritten the script and given Himself a happier ending. But He didn't. Instead, He denied Himself and kept trusting in His Father's plan.

All-in faith means forging forward in the face of adversity and choosing the righteous road over the facile freeway.

Selfishness can be a huge barrier when it comes to pursuing relationship with God. When we are more concerned about our own profit or pleasure rather than God's plans and purposes, our hearts and minds become compromised. That's what makes the life of Jesus so inspiring, because He was the most unselfish person to ever walk the earth. He didn't obsess over having everything go His way. He lived God's way.

If you struggle with selfish behaviors or tend to be self-absorbed, don't beat yourself up. You're not alone in your struggle, and change is possible! In my experience, when we choose to seek God more than we seek to have things go our way, something pretty amazing happens. The more we put God and others first, the more our perspective shifts. Instead of obsessing over our wants, needs, and problems, we're able to look beyond ourselves to see how God might be at work in the world around us. And the more we allow Him to open our eyes, the more courage we receive to move forward in faith.

So beloved, let's agree to put the obsession with self on a shelf in exchange for the pursuit of something greater than ourselves. Instead of seeking to have things go our way (and doing everything in our power to make sure they do), we can lift up our eyes and pray: *Jesus, let me be free of me so that all I see is You. Thy will be done. Thy will be done.*

3. Jesus craved to be in God's presence.

When Jesus was twelve years old, Mary and Joseph took him to Jerusalem for the Festival of the Passover, an annual celebration commemorating the Jews' escape from Egypt—when God delivered His people and set them free. After the festivities finished, Mary and Joseph headed back to Nazareth, not knowing that Jesus had stayed behind in Jerusalem.

Naturally, Jesus's parents were a little freaked out when they discovered he was not with them. For three days, they anxiously searched for him until they found him in the temple courts. I love Jesus's response to their anxiety in Luke 2:49, which also happens to be the first recorded words of Jesus in the entire Bible:

> "Why were you searching for me?" he asked. "Didn't you know I had to be in my Father's house?"

Wow. Simply amazing. Let's park on this verse for a minute so that we don't miss its significance.

Earlier in the chapter we talked about Jesus's last words before His ascension: "And surely I am with you always, to the very end of the age." These last words were centered on the gift of His presence and our ability as sons and daughters to access Him 24/7. Anytime, anyplace. How fitting that Jesus's first recorded words in Scripture also revolve around this idea of being in God's presence.

From beginning to end, Jesus lived a life of courageous faith that was marked by a constant pursuit of God's presence. What I love so much about this is that even though He and the Father were one (John 10:30), He still drew apart to connect with God in prayer—at all times! Even in His darkest hour in the garden He craved God's presence. And on the cross He grieved the loss of God's presence as He paid the ultimate price to erase the debt created by sin (Matthew 27:46).

There is no greater place for us to be than in God's presence. David reminds us of this in Psalm 84:10:

> Better is one day in your courts
>> than a thousand elsewhere;
> I would rather be a doorkeeper in the house
> of my God
>> than dwell in the tents of the wicked.

Nothing on earth—no festival, date, special event, or appointment—comes close to being with God; and thanks to Jesus, whose death on the cross removed all barriers and reconciled us to God, we do not have to be in a temple to experience His presence. We can experience Him whenever and wherever we please because He sent His very Spirit to live in us after He went to be with the Father. But, like Jesus, we have to want to be in God's presence. We have to choose and seek His presence above all else.

5. *Jesus kept His eyes fixed on the Father.*

I wish I could go back to life before cell phones and technology—life before it was sabotaged by a barrage of constant distraction. I may be a millennial, but I didn't have a cell phone until I was a sophomore in high school. And the older I get, the more thankful I am for my hands-free childhood.

As children, my sister and I baked, painted, played with dolls, biked outside, and built castles made of building blocks. We also read the Bible and fairy tales to each other before we went to bed. All these activities required us to concentrate on the task at hand, but keeping our eyes fixed on the task at hand wasn't difficult because we didn't have distractions. I think about trying to do those things today as an adult, and I don't know if I would even make it ten minutes without something buzzing or a light flashing in my face from my computer or cell phone. Full transparency: I struggled with constant Netflix distractions and temptations while writing this book. It's easier to be distracted by something bright, shiny, easy, and entertaining than to focus on something important that requires our attention. So sad but totally true, especially in this day and age.

I can only imagine the concentration Jesus must have had in order to keep putting one foot in front of the other after He was arrested. When the council of religious leaders condemned Him, when the Roman soldiers mocked Him, when He was led away to be crucified, when He was placed on the cross, Jesus kept His eyes firmly fixed on the Father and His perfect plan.

Jesus's commitment to the pursuit of God brings me to my knees and makes me want to hide my face like Isaiah, who said, "Woe to me!...I am ruined! For I am a man of unclean lips" (Isaiah 6:5). Woe to me, for I am not as committed to the pursuit of God as I ought to be. Yet the good news is that God never stops pursuing me—and you! Knowing this should encourage us to continue pursuing Him. The more we do, the deeper our faith will become as we begin to recognize the ways He is revealing Himself to us day after day after day.

Psalm 63 is a passage of Scripture I turn to regularly to join David in prayer, especially when I'm struggling to recognize and feel the presence of God. Say the words out loud with me now, paying attention to how your spirit feels before and after reading the psalm:

> You, God, are my God,
> > earnestly I seek you;
> I thirst for you,
> > my whole being longs for you,
> in a dry and parched land
> > where there is no water.
>
> I have seen you in the sanctuary
> > and beheld your power and your
> > glory.
> Because your love is better than life,
> > my lips will glorify you.
> I will praise you as long as I live,
> > and in your name I will lift up my hands.
> I will be fully satisfied as with the richest of
> foods;
> > with singing lips my mouth will
> > praise you.
>
> On my bed I remember you;
> > I think of you through the watches of
> > the night.
> Because you are my help,
> > I sing in the shadow of your wings.

I cling to you;
> your right hand upholds me.

Those who want to kill me will be de-
stroyed;
> they will go down to the depths of the
> earth.
They will be given over to the sword
> and become food for jackals.

But the king will rejoice in God;
> all who swear by God will glory in him,
> while the mouths of liars will be
> silenced.

If you're in a place where God seems silent today, let me encourage you to keep pursuing Him anyway. Don't stop because you haven't yet felt His presence or heard Him speak. He is at work. He is near.

GOING DEEPER

1. What is your morning routine? How can you be more intention-al about seeking God from the moment you open your eyes and throughout the day?

2. God does not always speak loudly; oftentimes He speaks to us in a whisper (1 Kings 19:11-12). What is one way you can create space in your day-to-day life to get away with God and listen for His still, small voice?

3. Be honest with yourself: What do you crave more than anything in the world? Do you crave to be in God's presence? Why or why not? What can you do to increase your hunger for God?

4. God is always with us, but it certainly doesn't always feel like it, does it? What are some ways you can practically look for Him in the midst of your daily routine?

PRAYER

Reread Psalm 63 as a prayer to God. Ask Him to grow in you a hunger to pursue Him above all else.

CHAPTER SEVEN

Building Endurance

Blessed is the one who perseveres under trial because,
having stood the test, that person will receive the crown of life
that the Lord has promised to those who love him.

—James 1:12

On August 6, 1926, at 7:08 a.m. British summer time, while most Americans lay sound asleep in their beds, Gertrude "Trudy" Ederle stood before the English Channel, covered in lard and petroleum and ready to tackle the challenge of a lifetime. She'd failed to become the first woman to swim across the Channel the year before, after her coach mistakenly took a resting floating position as a sign of distress and pulled the Olympic swimmer out. But Trudy wasn't going to make that same mistake again. No. With a new coach by her side and another year of training under her belt, Trudy was bound and determined to make history if it was the last thing she did.

The water was predictably cold, hence the need for lard and petroleum; but to everyone's surprise, it was also calm. At first, that is. But several hours into her swim, Trudy encountered a series of life-threatening squalls—one at noon and another at 6:00 p.m. The waves were so horrible that her coach, Bill Burgess, urged her to give up from a nearby boat. However, Trudy's father and sister, who accompanied Burgess in the boat, encouraged her to keep swimming.

As the story goes, Trudy's dad had promised her a new roadster if she accomplished the feat; and for added motivation, he reminded her of this prize when the swells began to rage. And so, Trudy swam on.

Fourteen hours and thirty-four minutes after her first step into the water on the beaches of Cape Gris-Nez, France, Ederle became the first woman and sixth person to successfully overcome the Channel. If these accomplishments weren't enough, she also smashed the records of the men who had gone before her. One small step for Trudy, and one giant leap for womankind, if you ask me.

What happened next is my favorite moment of this entire historic event. After Trudy reached the shores of Kingsdown in Kent, England, the entire world sat in wonder and awe over her seemingly impossible accomplishment. I can imagine many of them wanted to know how she did it. When the *New York Times* came knocking on her door, Trudy's response was simply, "I just knew if it could be done…it had to be done, and I did it."[1] But a later cable to her mother revealed that there was more to the story behind her success:

> We did it, Mother! We did it! The trick is turned and aren't you just so proud? We are all so happy. England and France are rejoicing in the glory. Oh, what crowds follow us here and there! The paper people are just impossible, but grand.
>
> Mom, I had that feeling of sure success—just wouldn't give up. Not once was I on the point of abandoning the swim. The good God led me on safely.[2]

Amazing, right? Trudy's words inspire me so much that I actually paraphrased the last three sentences on a sticky note in my office: "Never give up. Just keep swimming. The good God will lead you on."

Just keep swimming. It's amazing what power three simple words can have in our lives. These words helped Gertrude Ederle overcome the English Channel. In the animated movie *Finding Nemo*, these same words helped Marlin and Dory journey across the Pacific Ocean to find Nemo in Sydney, Australia. And with a little effort, strategy, and intentionality, they can help you and me to survive the deep waters of life. When it comes to going deeper in our faith in God, endurance is essential. Let's consider how we can build endurance in our faith walk.

Commit to Train

When my husband and I bought our first house in Savage, Minnesota, we strategically chose one close to the only nearby gym with a pool. Shortly after we became members, they began advertising for the gym's annual Commitment Day 5K run and walk. Hosted on New Year's Day every year, the family-friendly event allows members to commit to working toward a more fit and healthy lifestyle. While I've never participated in a Commitment Day 5K, I love the meaning behind the race and the message it sends to the world.

Regular exercise is important for building strength and endurance. The smarter and more often we train, the stronger we become and the more endurance we possess. But we have to commit. We have to say yes to the invitation to train—day in and day out.

The same principles apply to swimming with Jesus through the deep waters of life. The question is not whether or not we can overcome the waves and other challenges. The question is, will we commit to keep swimming, day in and day out, and trust that God will give us the strength and endurance we need to keep moving forward as we stay surrendered to Him?

Before we can start building endurance in faith, we have to commit to train, like my sweet friend Mary Ann, who is fifty-six years old and recently completed her first Half Ironman Triathlon. Now, I'm not calling Mary Ann old, but if crossing the finish line at that age (and beyond) is not amazing, I don't know what is! At her age, I'll be thankful if I've managed to put off having surgery on my joints and can still be active, period. I am honored to call Mary Ann friend; she is truly a modern Wonder Woman. But don't just take it from me. Take it from her peak training schedule:

Monday:	2 hours and 30 minutes of running (approximately 12.5 miles)
Tuesday:	30 minutes of strength training; 2,500-yard speed swim
Wednesday:	1 hour of indoor cycling
Thursday:	1 hour of speed drill running
Friday:	Strength training; 3,300-yard endurance swim
Saturday:	Brick workout, working the cycling into running transition (which is very difficult on the legs due to lactic acid build up); 75-mile outdoor bike ride into a quick transition 30-minute run (about 4.5 hours)
Sunday:	Rest

For twenty-eight weeks, Mary Ann committed her mind and body to this kind of rigorous training, and her commitment did not end after her lifting, swimming, biking, and running sessions were over. She had to eat, sleep, work, and take care of her body and mind like a champion—not only when she felt like it, but every single day.

Recently Mary Ann and I talked by phone about her experience of training for and competing in the Augusta 70.3 Ironman. She will be the first to tell you it was not an easy journey. Each week posed its own tears, challenges, setbacks, and heartbreaks. But Mary Ann stayed the course; and now, looking back, she says she never regretted doing a training session.

"One of the things I learned from all of this is that building endurance is really just about always moving forward," she told me. "The progress is never linear, but the goal is to keep working toward the finish line, whatever that finish line may be."

In the end, Mary Ann's training paid off as she crossed the finish line in 6:45:20—1,565 out of 3,314 athletes and 26 in her division. But the lessons she learned far surpass the realm of sports nutrition and endurance. As she shared with me in a recent email, "Competing in the Ironman proved once again that with God, truly all things are possible. When we trust in Him and seek to honor Him in all that we do, He is faithful!"[3]

Like Mary Ann trained for the triathlon, we must commit to train for a deep, courageous faith. We do this by living intentionally, pursuing God, and following what Scripture instructs followers of Jesus Christ to do.

In this area of commitment, our job is not to memorize as many verses and say as many prayers as we can. Our job is to trust, obey, and walk in a manner worthy of the calling to which we have been called (Ephesians 4:1 ESV).

Whether we realize it or not, committing to train and go deeper in faith honors God, for we know that without faith it is impossible to please God (Hebrews 11:6). As the days and years pass, our level of commitment will determine the level of endurance we produce.

Suit Up

The Bible calls us to suit up for the deep waters of life's journey. Just as an Olympic swimmer would never line up behind the starting blocks without a swimsuit, cap, and goggles, so we as people of faith should not get out of bed without first putting on our faith suit, which is the full armor of God: the belt of truth, breastplate of righteousness, shoes of peace, shield of faith, helmet of salvation, and sword of the Spirit (Ephesians 6:10-18). Why? Because it's our training gear and the key to building long-term endurance. Yet many of us go about our days wearing nothing more than a T-shirt and jeans!

Our job is not to memorize as many verses and say as many prayers as we can. Our job is to trust, obey, and walk in a manner worthy of the calling to which we have been called.

Sure, it's fun to talk about the armor of God, but how many of us actually suit up to face the day with faith before it's already underway? I confess there are days when I'm more apt to reach for my cell phone than I am to pray, *Lord, help me be strong in you and your mighty armor and power today.*

But my days of swimming through life ill-equipped and unprepared for battle are over. I know what it's like to disregard the armor and not apply it to my life. I've been down that dismal road, and I'm not going back.

Beloved, battles are won and lost by our decision to wear or leave behind the armor God has instructed us to hold fast to. If we are going to build endurance, we have to suit up—to put on our faith suit. Let's unpack what this means.

Belt of Truth

The first item of our faith suit that we must put on is the belt of truth (Ephesians 6:14). Why a belt? What's the significance behind it? When the apostle Paul wrote this illustration thousands of years ago, a belt was a crucial part of a Roman soldier's armor because it held all the other pieces in place. Most scholars agree that without it, a soldier could not be effective in battle.

Likewise, as we swim through the deep waters of life, we need to arm ourselves with God's truth—the only thing that can truly hold us together and cut through the enemy's deception and schemes. Practically speaking, here's what this looks like for me on a daily basis:

- I pray Romans 12:2 over myself, asking God to transform me by the renewing of my mind so that I may be able to discern His pleasing and perfect will.
- I spend at least ten minutes reading the Bible and asking God to help me align all areas of my life to the gold standard of His truth.
- I take every thought, circumstance, and spoken word captive to Christ (2 Corinthians 10:5), filtering it through the truths found in His Word.

I don't always get things right, but I've learned that the more I seek to secure myself with the belt of God's truth, the more equipped I am to face the waves. For when we know the truth, we are set free (John 8:32). Free to swim. Free to fight. Free to overcome.

Breastplate of Righteousness

Before speaking at an event last year, I met my sister and a friend for lunch at one of my favorite bakeries. If sharing time with these two special people didn't add enough sweetness to my life, the almond croissants and macaroons sure sent my joy meter over the top.

After saying grace, my friend immediately turned her face to meet mine. Her eyes brimmed with excitement, and I could tell she had a lot on her mind.

"So, what's new with you, lady?" I asked. With me having moved to North Carolina, it had been months since we'd exchanged a text, let alone met for lunch.

Passion flooded her eyes as she opened her mouth to speak.

"I've got to tell you, Lauren, something incredible has happened in my faith journey," she said. "I may be a gramma, but for the first time in my life, I feel like I've finally realized what it means to claim the righteousness available to us in Jesus! I'm braver and bolder than ever!"

The joy in her face was palpable and contagious. I smiled from ear to ear as she continued to talk about what the Lord had been teaching her since we last connected.

This woman had known Christ from the time she was a little girl. She had prayed to Him, read His Word, and proclaimed the good news around town. But it wasn't until decades later that she finally picked up the breastplate of righteousness, which Paul mentions in Ephesians 6:14, and wore it for herself. What exactly is righteousness? I love how Priscilla Shirer puts it: "Truth provides the grid; righteousness paints the picture. Righteousness is right living—walking 'in a manner worthy of the calling with which you have been called' (Ephesians 4:1)."[4]

We can live right because of the gift of righteousness. We can put off our old self and put on the very righteousness of Christ because God made a way for us to do just that: "God made him who had no sin to be sin for us, so that in him we might become the righteousness of God" (2 Corinthians 5:21). This wardrobe change is possible only because of Jesus's work on the cross.

Just as a Roman soldier's heart was protected when he put on a breastplate, our hearts are protected from the enemy's attacks when we put on the breastplate of righteousness—when we rest in knowing that Jesus gives us the ability to live as we are called to live.

Shoes of Peace

Our feet provide a foundation for our entire body. When we stand, the forefoot, midfoot, and hindfoot bones must work together, along with all of the conjoining muscles, tendons, and ligaments. Perhaps one of the most fascinating pieces of foot anatomy is the Achilles tendon. As the largest and strongest tendon in the human body, the Achilles tendon connects the heel bone to the muscles at the back of the calf. It's what enables us to stand, walk, run, and dance. No Achilles, no movement. Period.

I like to think about the shoes of peace as the Achilles tendon of the faith suit. They are our firm foundation. When our feet are fitted with the gospel of peace—the good news of God's peace in Christ—we are grounded, fully prepared for battle. But without the shoes? We're incapacitated, prone to be devoured by the fears constantly swirling all around us.

There is a peace that surpasses all understanding, and this peace comes only from God Himself—guarding our hearts and minds in Christ (Philippians 4:7). I, for one, would trade every pair of fashionable boots and heels I own if that was necessary for me to wear the shoes of peace for the rest of my life. But because of Christ, I *can* wear these shoes every day.

In the days when Paul preached, a Roman soldier's shoes were different from the sandals worn by your average Roman citizen. The shoe itself was made of leather and metal, and the bottoms were outfitted with sharp spikes, designed to help the soldier have firm footing when navigating uneven terrain or engaging in combat.

Just like the Roman soldiers, we put on these shoes to prepare ourselves for whatever we might encounter on any given day. And when the enemy tries to push us around, we stand firm and trust God's peace to hold us in place.

I had the opportunity to practice this yet again this spring when the monster of pain, anxiety, and depression started to rear its ugly head as it usually does around that time of the year. While the old Lauren would have gone into what I like to call the "panic, woe-is-me mode," I've been around the block and spent enough time in God's Word to know He will give me peace for the storm when I fit my feet with the gospel of peace, which is the blood of Christ, poured out to make us one with the Father and to break down the dividing wall of hostility (Ephesians 2:14).

True peace comes from knowing God is with us and for us, fighting on our behalf and working all things together for our good.

True peace comes from knowing God is with us and for us, fighting on our behalf and working all things together for our good.

There is no greater gear to help us stand our ground and keep moving forward than the shoes of peace. The seas will rage; but when we concentrate on God and His promises instead of the chaos, we will receive the peace we need to carry us through the storm.

Shield of Faith

All of the attributes of faith we talked about in chapter 5—following wholeheartedly after Jesus, daring to believe, resting in God's promises, asking for provision, and resolving to persevere—make up the shield of faith. As Paul writes in Ephesians 6:16, this shield enables us to "extinguish all the flaming arrows of the evil one," much as it enabled Roman soldiers to thwart off enemy darts and arrows as their primary tool of defense.

The enemy's arrows or darts cannot harm us, because our confidence and hope are in God and His promise to protect us. This promise is beautifully expressed in Psalm 91, one of my favorite passages of all time:

> He will cover you with his feathers,
>> and under his wings you will find refuge;
>> his faithfulness will be your shield and
>> rampart.
> You will not fear the terror of night,
>> nor the arrow that flies by day,
> nor the pestilence that stalks in the darkness,
>> nor the plague that destroys at midday.
> A thousand may fall at your side,
>> ten thousand at your right hand,
>> but it will not come near you.
> You will only observe with your eyes
>> and see the punishment of the wicked.
> If you say, "The LORD is my refuge,"
>> and you make the Most High your dwelling,
> no harm will overtake you,
>> no disaster will come near your tent.
>
> (vv. 4-10)

God's faithfulness enables us to have faith, thus becoming our shield and rampart that protects us from any danger threatening to knock us out or pull us under.

Helmet of Salvation

The next item in our faith suit is the helmet of salvation (Ephesians 6:17). In Paul's day, when a Roman soldier suited up for battle, the helmet was the last piece to be put in place. But this finishing touch wasn't just the cherry on top of the soldier's protective uniform. Without the helmet, all other pieces rendered themselves useless in battle. After all, it would take only one blow to the head to be knocked out for good.

Spiritually speaking, the helmet of salvation also guards our minds from fatal blows and helps us remember the victory Christ has already given us through the gift of salvation. Once we put our life into His hands and move from the undercurrents of despair into His currents of love, we are saved—now and forever. And once we receive this gift, nothing and no one can take it away from us. We are sons and daughters of the ultimate Deliverer.

> No blow will be fatal for the one whose home is in heaven.

We put on the helmet of salvation each day as we remember the price Christ paid for our freedom and righteousness. He shed His blood, died, and rose again so that we wouldn't have to fear death. Because guess what? He has already conquered it for us! Because of the salvation we have been given, we are protected, forgiven, and free. No blow will be fatal for the one whose home is in heaven.

Sword of the Spirit

In high school, I traveled with our Spanish Club on a seven-day tour of Spain, France, and Great Britain. While I certainly enjoyed running down the steps of the Eiffel Tower, eating chocolate-hazelnut spread and croissants for breakfast, and seeing the guards at Buckingham Palace, Spain is the country I loved most. Forget leaving your heart in San Francisco. I left mine in the streets, palaces, and museums of Madrid, Seville, Granada, Toledo, and Málaga.

Of all the cities we visited in Spain, Toledo was the most enchanting. I still remember the wonder I felt the moment our tour bus pulled up to the Mirador del Valle, a scenic overlook offering a panoramic view of the city on a hill and the Tajo River beneath it. I've climbed mountains and monuments, but nothing compares to the view from Mirador del Valle. One look at the majestic and historic hills of Toledo, and you feel like you've walked into the pages of an old fairy tale storybook.

But the view is only half of what makes Toledo truly unique. As our tour guide explained, the city's other claim to fame comes from its creation of Toledo steel, known historically as unusually hard steel. She said that since around 500 BC, Toledo has been one of the largest traditional sword-making, steel-working centers in the world. Famed for its high-quality alloy, Roman legions favored Toledo weaponry over competing Damascus and Samurai steel methods. I don't know how to wield an actual sword, but goodness, did I feel powerful holding a Toledo steel Excalibur replica in my hand. As I ran my fingers up and down the smooth blade, I couldn't help wondering if the Roman soldiers of Paul's day used weapons forged from the very same city.

Here's what I love about the last piece of armor in our faith suit. The sword of the Spirit is like having a Toledo steel Excalibur strapped to us every single day. And we don't have to take sword fighting lessons or spend hours building muscle in the gym to learn how to wield it. All we have to do is follow Paul's advice in Ephesians 6:17 and simply take up the sword of the Spirit, which is the word of God—not just when we feel like it or when the enemy strikes, but every day to build endurance. The more knowledgeable we are about the Word, the more able we are to use it to protect and defend ourselves and others.

We must renew our mind with truth every single day, because the more truth we know, the easier it is to recognize and defeat a lie when one tries to take us down. As Paul instructs us to do in 2 Corinthians 10:5, we must "demolish arguments and every pretension that sets itself up against the knowledge of God, and we take captive every thought to make it obedient to Christ."

Beloved, I don't know what thoughts are currently plastered across your mind's landscape, but if they don't line up with God's Word, they will not serve you well in times of battle. Do you know what the Bible says about you? Do you try to spend time in the Bible daily—not just so you can check it off your to-do list but so you can be equipped for righteous, victorious living? I promise you, you will never regret making the choice to get more familiar with God's Word and fill your mind with its truths.

We build endurance for the deep waters of life when we choose to suit up with faith every single day, because then and only then can we "be strong in the Lord and in His mighty power" (Ephesians 6:10). Our strength is not sufficient to resist and overcome sin's curse. This is why the apostle Paul tells us to "put on the full armor of God, so that you can take your stand against the devil's schemes" (Ephesians 6:11). It is only when we are armed and ready in Christ that, "when the day of evil comes, [we will] be able to stand [our] ground, and after [we] have done everything, to stand" (Ephesians 6:13).

The issue is not whether or not we have access to a faith suit. That question was answered at the cross! Jesus conquered death and gives us truth, righteousness, peace, faith, salvation, and power to protect us and keep us safe—even in the worst of storms. The only question that remains is whether or not we will equip ourselves with the faith suit we need to just keep swimming.

For Gertrude Ederle it was lard, petroleum, goggles, a cap, and a suit. For Mary Ann, it was a tri suit and sneakers. For us, it's a faith suit.

The only question is: will you commit to train? The gear is ready and waiting for you, and you don't even need to enter your credit card information to pick it up. So what are you waiting for? It's time to suit up.

GOING DEEPER

1. What aspect of the faith suit is easiest for you to put on every day, and why? Which is hardest, and why?

2. How would you explain to someone in your own words what it means to commit to train and put on the faith suit each day? How can this help build the endurance we need to just keep swimming?

3. Do you believe in the power of God's Word? If so, how have you experienced the power of God's Word in different areas of your life?

4. Reflect on a recent or current battle. How did or how could the faith suit help you keep your head above the waves?

5. Which items of the faith suit are you most in need of today? Most thankful for today?

PRAYER

Lord, thank You for giving me access to Your divine power. Thank You for the gift of the faith suit and all the protection and power it gives me to stand firm against the enemy's schemes. Help me commit to train and put the suit on every single day of my life so that I can build endurance in faith to survive and thrive in the deep. I want to wear and wield the belt of truth, breastplate of righteousness, shoes of peace, shield of faith, helmet of salvation, and sword of the Spirit each day so that I can become stronger in YOU. Make me stronger in You, Father, even today. In Jesus's name. Amen.

CHAPTER EIGHT

Overcoming Your Deepest Fears

*Fear is a self-imposed prison that will keep you
from becoming what God intends for you to be.
You must move against it with the weapons of faith and love.*

—Rick Warren[1]

I am a water girl through and through, but just thinking about the creatures that might lurk in Davy Jones's locker makes me break out in a cold sweat. I've always been afraid of monsters, particularly those of the aquatic kind.

When we were kids, my sister, cousins, and I weren't afraid to swim in the channels of our grandparents' lake. That is, until we found out we weren't swimming alone.

One sunny afternoon we decided to paddle our boats over to the island in the middle of the lake just beyond our grandparents' channel. After reaching the destination, we dragged the inflatable watercrafts onto shore where we snacked on Goldfish crackers before swimming around the island.

"You can't catch me!" I yelled to my cousins as I swam farther away from shore. Everyone knew I was the fastest swimmer of the bunch, and not having eaten my slice of humble pie for the day, I happily rubbed it in their faces. But my excitement was short lived, because seconds later I noticed something eerie happening in the water nearby.

"What's that?" I asked, pointing to the ripple that was inching its way closer to my cousin.

"Snake! Snake! Snake!" my sister shouted as she stood up and ran for the island.

Panic quickly consumed us all, and before we knew it, we found ourselves in our boats and had paddled all the way back to our grandparents' house. Needless to say, after learning about water snakes, muskrats, and all the other scary creatures that swam in the lake, I didn't really want to be in the water anymore.

Snakes aren't just found in lakes, oceans, and other dark waters; they are found in Scripture too. If you flip through the Old Testament, you will find several references to the ancient sea serpent, Leviathan. I dare you to Google *Leviathan* and click on images. I mean, seriously. This is not a beast to be trifled with. We're talking sharp fangs, scales, tendrils, claws, and just about any other frightening feature you can think of all rolled up into one being.

Isaiah 27:1 in the New International Version describes Leviathan as "the gliding…coiling serpent"—a monster of the sea. Other translations refer to him as "the dragon who *lives* in the sea" (NASB) and "the piercing...crooked serpent" (KJV). I love how Jonathan Martin interprets Leviathan in his book *How to Survive a Shipwreck*: "Leviathan represented everything about the world that is disordered, disorienting, and frightening to human sensibilities. In a word, Leviathan represented chaos—the primal forces at work in the cosmos that we cannot know or understand, much less domesticate or control."[2]

Martin seems to be describing everything that opposes God. Evil itself.

What makes the deep so unnerving is that we cannot see what is lurking beneath us until it's right beneath our feet. Likewise, we cannot see or know when we might encounter evil—when or how the enemy of our souls might strike.

After I surfaced from what I would call my first high sea battle—unexplained pain and resulting anxiety and depression that ultimately caused a crisis of faith, which peaked in college—I became very aware of the enemy's agenda to steal, kill, and destroy (John 10:10). And while I've come a long way since those dark days, last year it all seemed to be returning once again.

I had always feared relapsing, and now my worst nightmare was coming true. But not only was it coming true, I felt like there was nothing I could do to stop it. In the dark of night when the waves of anxiety hovered over me like an unwanted specter, I sensed the serpent swimming right below me, taunting me with an attack on my faith. *Where is God now?* he would say.

My body tensed as I tried to swim away from the danger I sensed in my thought life. What if I end up as anxious and depressed as I was in high school and college? What if I get caught in the undertow again and I don't make it out this time? What if I never feel like myself again?

I didn't know if I would have the strength to keep swimming if the seas became that rough again. Sure, I had learned to swim with Jesus, but what if I somehow lost my ability to trust Him and spiraled into the abyss again? These fears plagued me on and off for months.

When we overcome our first high-sea battle with the help of Jesus, our immediate reaction is always relief. Whew, we made it! We are so grateful to our Savior and often comforted by the calmer waters. But I have found that in the aftermath of a battle, fear quickly follows our reprieve.

Something triggers a memory, and we cringe as we remember the pain and heartbreak we experienced. We look around and notice that even though the waters are calmer, they are still dark—full of unknowns and an enemy who wants to destroy us and the trust we have in our Savior. And so we fear the what-ifs? We wonder what will happen if the enemy stirs up the waters and we are pulled into the undercurrent again. We need a plan for how to handle our deepest fears and the battles of the deep.

What Happens When Our Worst Nightmares Come to Life?

In the Book of Job we are introduced to a man whose life was plagued with multiple attacks from the enemy. Scripture tells us he was a wealthy man who also had a big family. Because of his prosperity, Job owned thousands of sheep, camels, donkeys, and oxen—not to mention servants to cater to his every need (Job 1:3). We also know that he was a good man: "blameless and upright; he feared God and shunned evil" (Job 1:1). Yet God allowed Satan to test Job by "stirring up the waters" and stripping away his wealth, children, livestock, and servants (Job 1:13-19). In my Bible, this chapter of the book is appropriately titled "Job Loses Everything."

What the enemy intends to harm us, God can and will use for good.

What amazes and inspires me every time I read this story is that even after such excruciating devastation, this man of God ultimately did not "drown" or lose his faith. It's a heartbreaking story, but for me the outcome is liberating. Job's story reminds us that God does not cause suffering. While He may allow it and use it to purify our faith and draw us deeper into relationship with Him, He does not allow the enemy to overcome us.

What the enemy intends to harm us, God can and will use for good.

Yes, "we are more than conquerors through him who loved us" (Romans 8:37).

God is stronger than the enemy beneath our feet, and He has a divine check on the chaos that the enemy's movement creates. Even if our worst nightmare comes to life, God is not surprised; and if we can just hold on, we will see deliverance once again.

Nothing has proven this truth to me more than when I was experiencing my relapse, because even though I didn't think I had what it took to make it through to the other side, the faith and relationship I'd been cultivating with God allowed me to stand my ground, stronger than ever before. For the first time I realized that because of my strengthened faith, I didn't have to fall back into the undertow I had been sucked into in high school and college. I didn't have to fear the attacks of the enemy anymore, because God had already given me the victory. And He would give it to me this time too. Even if I couldn't control what was happening in my brain or my body, I knew I could choose to keep my eyes fixed on Jesus and keep swimming with Him—because He who is strong to save us once is strong to save us for the rest of our lives.

As scary as this time was, deep down in my soul I believe God used this experience to help me overcome my fear of the enemy and reaffirm the power of the faith I'd found in my Rescuer.

The fight wasn't easy. Let me tell you, waking up with three panic attacks a night, having shaking fits, and sinking in and out of depression and anxiety all day long are things I never wanted to experience. These were some of the darkest, hardest days of my life. I wouldn't wish them on anyone. I was so broken and exhausted that even simple things like making a grocery list were hard. In the middle of one sleepless night, I remember wondering what was becoming of me. I wondered if I would ever feel like myself again. I wondered if I would ever fully enjoy life again. In those moments, I pulled out my battle plan and put into practice everything God had taught me since I first reached out to Him in faith. I've shared practices that are part of this plan in earlier chapters, but I hope and pray that condensing and presenting this four-step battle plan for you here will be a ready resource you can turn to and use to overcome whatever fears and battles you might face.

He who is strong to save us once is strong to save us for the rest of our lives.

The Faithful Swimmer's Battle Plan

Just because we have faith and have survived a battle doesn't mean we won't face another one at some point or another. But we don't have to fear the enemy or the waves that come crashing over us. All we need is the right battle plan to keep swimming.

1. Remember the 3 Ps

In chapter 5 we learned the three Ps of a deeper faith: promises, provision, and perseverance. Those same principles apply here. When we are tempted to fear that we aren't going to be strong enough to keep swimming, we must remember the first two Ps, God's promises and provision, some of which I am listing again here for easy reference:

- He gives strength to those who are weary and power to those who are weak. (Isaiah 40:29)
- When we pass through deep waters, He is with us. The waves will not sweep over us. (Isaiah 43:2)
- No weapon formed against us will prevail. (Isaiah 54:17)
- He will never leave us or forsake us. (Deuteronomy 31:8)
- His plans are to give us a hope and a future. (Jeremiah 29:11)
- He has not given us a Spirit of fear but of power, love, and a sound mind. (2 Timothy 1:7 KJV)
- When we call out to God, He delivers us from our troubles. (Psalm 34:17)
- He is working all things together for our good. (Romans 8:28)
- He loves us with an everlasting love—a love that endures forever. (Psalm 136:26)
- He will supply our every need. (Philippians 4:19)

The God who loves and protects you is the same God who breaks the heads of Leviathan (Psalm 74:13). He is not subject to the enemy; the enemy is subject to God. And when we recall this divine authority, we are given the hope we need to persevere—the third P.

When you're in the midst of a battle and need to keep swimming, say these verses and truths out loud so that you take them in, making them your own.

2. Keep Your Faith Suit On

Remember all the daily practices we learned to build endurance in chapter 7—putting on the belt of truth, breastplate of righteousness, shoes of peace, shield of faith, helmet of salvation, and the sword of the Spirit? These same practices apply when we need to keep swimming! In fact, never has it been more important to live out Paul's instructions in Ephesians 6 regarding the armor of God than when we're in the midst of a battle. Don't take off the belt of truth. Keep wearing the breastplate of righteousness and the shoes of peace. Pick up that shield of faith and fasten your helmet of salvation. As a child of God, you've learned to sharpen your sword, the Word of God. And dear friend, now is your time to use it.

3. Huddle Up

As a swim teacher, I didn't just teach kids how to swim; I taught them how to survive if they ever found themselves in life-threatening situations. Aside from wearing life jackets, one of the skills the American Red Cross recommends kids learn is how to find safety and rest in a huddle if they start to get cold or weak in the water.

The reasoning behind it is this: the longer we are left alone in cold, rough waters, the less chance we have of survival. As our core body temperature drops and we become weak, heat loss hits our extremities and then our vital organs and brain. But a group of two or more people can adopt the huddle position to conserve heat.

In a huddle, swimmers form a circle by reaching out to the people around them and linking arms and legs together in a tight, chain-like configuration. This position not only helps stranded swimmers conserve heat but also prevents people from drifting away into oblivion. While huddling, swimmers are encouraged to talk to each other and maintain an upbeat outlook.

When I look back on the battle I faced after my hEDS diagnosis and the return of the anxiety monster, I know I wouldn't have endured the conditions if I hadn't reached out to my brothers and sisters in Christ who, praise the Lord, were willing to link arms and brave the battle with me.

The enemy of our souls wants to isolate us. He wants us to tremble in fear—to feel lonely and helpless. But, oh, what help is available when we are bold enough to reach out to both God and others!

One of my favorite examples of the huddle in action is found in Luke 1:26-56, where Elizabeth links arms with Mary after she learns that she will be the mother of Jesus. Let's watch what happens after Mary hears the big news. Naturally she is shocked, but instead of panicking, she asks the angel to explain himself a little more.

> The angel answered, "The Holy Spirit
> will come on you, and the power
> of the Most High will overshadow
> you.…Even Elizabeth your relative
> is going to have a child in her old age,
> and she who was said to be unable to
> conceive is in her sixth month." (Luke
> 1:35-36)

What we learn from the angel is that not only did Mary have the power of the Holy Spirit *in* her, but she also had a "sister" who could come *alongside* her to encourage her to have faith. So Mary did what every faithful swimmer should do and headed toward Elizabeth's house for encouragement.

If I had to guess, Mary probably felt overwhelmed, confused, and afraid on her journey to see Elizabeth. Regardless of how she may have been feeling, when she made it to her destination, the Holy Spirit gave Elizabeth a greeting that encouraged Mary to have faith:

> "Blessed are you among women, and
> blessed is the child you will bear! But
> why am I so favored, that the mother
> of my Lord should come to me? As
> soon as the sound of your greeting
> reached my ears, the baby in my womb
> leaped for joy. Blessed is she who has
> believed that the Lord would fulfill his
> promises to her!" (Luke 1:42-45)

We don't know all the details of this exchange or what thoughts might have been going through Mary's head when she heard Elizabeth's greeting, but it must have strengthened Mary's faith, because one verse later Mary erupts into a song of praise. At the end of the song, we learn that Mary stays with Elizabeth for three more months.

Sometimes all we need is a reaffirming word from a brother or sister in Christ. But we will never get the support we need if we don't set our pride and fear aside and reach out for help.

4. Pull Out the SOS File

This aspect of the battle plan is something I borrowed from one of my best friends and ministry partners, Heather Dixon, who also happens to be a fellow writer and hEDS warrior. She calls it the Code Red file, but because we are in the deep, I've affectionately renamed it the SOS File.

If you're in the middle of a battle right now, it's not too late to create an SOS file; and if you're not in the middle of a battle, this section is meant to encourage you to be proactive so that your file is ready to go when the time comes.

When I was diagnosed with hEDS and my anxiety flared, I called Heather in tears, hoping to receive some reassurance and advice. After praying over me, she asked me if I had an SOS file.

"A what?" I replied.

"An SOS file! You know, something you keep in your house that's full of things to help you get through battles," she said.

Here are some examples of what can be included in the file:

- Mementos
- Cards from family and friends
- Words of encouragement
- Special prayers
- Favorite Scripture cards
- Favorite tea
- Favorite comfort snack
- Favorite comfort food recipes
- A list of answered prayers and praises
- A journal
- A worship CD or playlist
- Things that are true, noble, right, pure, lovely, and admirable (Philippians 4:8)
- Other things that make you smile or bring you hope

Pulling out our SOS file helps us move forward and keep our eyes above the waves when we find ourselves in challenging waters. The more we reflect on the contents of our file, the easier it is to keep a positive, faithful perspective. Instead of spiraling into fear, we can renew our minds by immersing ourselves with encouragement.

Choosing Faith over Fear

We are promised hardships in this life, but God uses them for good to build our faith and draw us deeper into Him. For every hardship, we are also promised peace and victory (John 16:33; Romans 8:28).

If we know God is sovereign over the enemy lurking beneath our feet, and if we have the right battle plan in place to face the waves when he stirs things up, what then do we have to be afraid of?

When we can stare Leviathan in the face and say, "I am not afraid of you! I am not afraid of what chaos you might inflict on me out here in the deep because I have a lifeguard, and His name is Jesus. I have a battle plan, and I am promised victory over your schemes," then we are free from the fear of the what-ifs.

I never wanted to face another battle with anxiety and depression like the one I faced in my youth. I used to shake with fear at the simple thought of it. But in His goodness, God liberated me from that fear by helping me to face and overcome one of my worst nightmares. Was it painful? You bet. Did it nearly take everything out of me? Absolutely. Would I choose to go through it again? Not a chance. But here's the beautiful thing: I'm still here. Like Job, I didn't drown—not once, not twice. Because of my faith, I finally possess the courage I need to face fear and overcome—something I never thought would be possible for me.

Today when the waves start to rise and fear starts to creep back into my life, I go into battle mode using the tactics I have outlined in this chapter. I declare God's promises over my life. I meditate on them daily in prayer, and I find comfort in remembering that He will provide my every need. I make sure I'm wearing the full armor of God. I reach out to the people around me who can help keep me warm and safe. And if I feel myself slipping into despair, I pull out my SOS file to help me keep my eyes fixed on what is true, noble, right, pure, lovely, and admirable. I have found that if

I engage all aspects of this battle plan, my faith is strengthened and I can overcome whatever Goliath I'm facing.

Fear is defeated when we choose to be a warrior instead of a worrier. I know this isn't always easy. Sometimes it's easier to give in to fear. But we have to fight in faith. We have to remember that the Jesus inside us is stronger than the darkness that threatens to overtake us. Greater is He who is in us than he who is in the world (1 John 4:4). When we remember and claim these truths for ourselves, the enemy loses his grip on us and we overcome his schemes.

> *Fear is defeated when we choose to be a warrior instead of a worrier.*

I don't know what battles I'll face days from now, let alone years from now, but what I know is this: Even if Leviathan comes back and stirs up a mighty tempest, I will be OK—because I have faith. I have a battle plan. And for the first time in my life, I am not afraid.

If you take away only one thing from this chapter, let it be this: dear friend, because you are equipped for battle, you have nothing to fear.

GOING DEEPER

1. What about swimming in the deep scares you the most? In other words, what are your deepest fears, and why?
2. What battles has God already helped you overcome, and what were the outcomes?
3 What might be keeping you from diving into a fearless faith?
4. What fears and lies do you need to let go of today?
5. What items will you put in your SOS file?

PRAYER

Lord, I've read that in You I have nothing to fear. Help me to believe this. Help me to overcome my fear of the enemy beneath my feet and the battles that the storm and waves may bring. Lord, I ask for courage to become the fearless swimmer You have always longed for me to be. Take my fears and fill me with Your holy strength, confidence, and peace. In Jesus's name. Amen.

CHAPTER NINE

Your Compass in the Deep

Where we go is not nearly as important as who we go with.

—*Suzanne Eller*[1]

I love ethnic food. Indian, Thai, Mediterranean, Mexican, Bahamian, Italian, Moroccan, you name it. I've lived in five states and seven cities, and while I can't tell you much about the local sports teams or civic arts of those cities, I can tell you where to find the best ethnic food.

On road trips I've been known to stop for curry, falafel, or street tacos when a craving strikes. My husband, Alex, affectionately calls these pit stops "wifey detours," and anything under fifteen miles is fair game. My favorite places to stop are Indian restaurants. There is nothing quite like the smell of Indian spices. Cardamom, cumin, saffron, fenugreek, cinnamon, garam masala, tamarind, curry, and ginger create the perfect balance of sweet and savory in every dish.

My only problem with Indian restaurants is, ironically, the menu.

Seriously, how is someone supposed to choose from seventy-five dishes when everything sounds good? It's impossible—a complete fool's errand, especially for someone like me who, half the time, can't make up her mind. All this indecision and wondering usually leads me to make the same decision every time. It's easier and much less stressful. There are no guessing games or surprises, and I am not disappointed. I order my Peshawari Naan and Chicken Saag, and I know exactly what I'm going to get.

Not long after discovering my love for ethnic food in college, I realized that making decisions in life is sometimes a lot like trying to order from an Indian restaurant. It can be puzzling, frustrating, exhausting, and burdensome. If we mull over a decision long enough, fatigue starts to settle in, slowly paralyzing us in the process. If we're not careful, often we'll end up choosing the safest, most familiar option—whatever makes the most sense at the time—because once fatigue sets in, we aren't in a place to truly care about the effects of the choices we make. So we fit right into the "flavor of the day," which is "Who cares? Just make a decision." When we do finally choose something, it's often not a choice of faith but of disbelief.

There have been times in my life when I've made decisions based on faith, trusting God, and others when I've made decisions without faith. In the case of the latter, they generally have been hastier decisions, when I just wanted the waiting and guessing game to be over. So I stopped waiting and listening and just did what made sense at the time. The difference between the two? Night and day! As you can probably guess, the outcomes were quite different too.

Rushed decisions often lead to more stress and problems—things that could be avoided if we would just be patient and wait on God's timing. On the other hand, patient, unhurried decisions that are surrendered to Christ usually bring peace and resolution.

Before Alex and I graduated from college, we set our hearts on moving to Minneapolis, where I had worked as an intern the summer before graduation. After praying about it, we felt confident about the move; but things got complicated when two companies offered me a job. To many, that might sound like a dream come true. But for me, it wasn't. Receiving two job offers only made me question and doubt what to do. I wondered how I was supposed to discern what position to take, and I felt a huge weight of pressure to make the right decision. One company offered me a paid internship at my favorite Minneapolis magazine publication. The other offered me a full-time job working in the communications department for a top suburban school district.

The magazine editors did not promise that the internship would lead to a full-time job, but that didn't affect my decision. I'd spent my entire undergraduate career working to become the editor-in-chief of our campus magazine. I loved everything about the world of publishing. As a magazine journalism major, I lived for storyboarding, interviewing, writing, late-night editing sessions, headline development, and design. The job decision should have been an easy one for me to make. Yet surprisingly, it wasn't.

I wrestled over the choice for days.

God, I'm so confused and I don't know what to do. I need Your help to make a decision. Please, show me Your will, I prayed.

Common sense told me to pick the magazine internship. Paid internships are few and far between; and if a publication pays, that usually means you have a shot at getting your foot in the door once you complete the internship. This was a dream come true—everything I had worked and hoped for. But in my prayer times, I did not have peace. My head wanted me to take the magazine position, but my heart said no.

It didn't make sense to me, but I could feel God pushing me in the direction of the school communications job. As I thought and prayed about that job, I could hear Him whispering Jeremiah 29:11 over me: "'For I know the plans I have for you,' declares the LORD, 'plans to prosper you and not to harm you, plans to give you hope and a future.'" In those moments of silent petition and reflection, I knew God was asking me to take a leap of faith. He didn't just want me to obey; He wanted me to trust His plan.

A few days later I gathered my family together to tell them what I had chosen.

"I don't know how to explain this," I began. "I feel like God is telling me to take the communications job. I know it doesn't make sense, and I know that means I'm potentially walking away from a career in the magazine industry, but I just don't have a peace about the internship."

By the time I finished talking, everyone's faces had expressions of shock. This didn't surprise me. I was just as shocked as they were. I didn't know what this decision would mean for my career or my life. I didn't know where God was leading me. I just knew it was the right decision to make, because when I called the magazine to decline, I was filled with overwhelming peace.

It was the first real decision I had ever made 100 percent by faith. At the time, I didn't know what God's purpose was in having me work at a school district, but in hindsight I can see that God had a purpose and a plan for my time there; and a lot of the skills I learned are skills I use in my ministry work today.

Of course, since that decision, I haven't always made patient, faithful decisions in every area of my life. But I'm getting better at surrendering the decision-making process to God and relying on Him to help me make a choice that honors Him. Instead of rushing into a decision, I've learned to pray, listen, wait, trust, and filter the messages I receive regarding the situation through God's Word. And you know what? The more I seek to honor God with the decisions I make, the more equipped I am to make the next decision by faith when it comes.

Whether we're deciding where to live or work, or whether we should take on another project, join an activity, or participate in a committee, many of the thousands of decisions we make each day require more than choosing the safe, sensible option or going with our gut. They require exercising faith—trusting that God will help us make the right decision as we seek and rely on Him. They require getting away from the noise and opinions of this world to get with the God who ordains our very steps. And the first step to making faith-filled decisions is to get on our knees and pray.

Pray Without Ceasing

When faced with a decision, my first instinct used to be to see what everyone else had to say about the situation. If I couldn't figure out how to deal with a friend who was drifting away from me, I called my sister before turning to God. If I wasn't sure if I should take a risk, I surveyed my friends and family to see what they thought before asking God. This is what the enemy wants—for us to be distracted and confused, for our minds to be filled with the opinions of others, for us not to be able to get away with the Lord in a set-aside time of prayer (as opposed to praying on the run as we often do). But as people of faith, we aren't supposed to pray just because God's Word tells us to. We are supposed to pray because it is actually beneficial to us!

I learned this the hard way. Many of my friends know me as the woman they can turn to when they need prayer or prayer advice, but it hasn't always been this way. There have been times in my life when prayer was more of an afterthought or last resort when things got really bad. There have been times when I wondered if God even heard my prayers. There have been times when I doubted the power of prayer. Maybe you can relate.

But in this journey of diving deeper into faith, I have discovered that prayer is an essential part of making faith-filled decisions. When we lift our hands up to the Father, when we pour our hearts out in honest surrender and faith, when we acknowledge God's sovereignty over our situation, when we pray believing God hears us and is going before us— strongholds start to break and, in Jesus's name, a shift takes place in our spiritual atmosphere.

You see, prayer isn't just powerful; it's also very effective (James 5:16). And we can know God is listening because His Word tells us that when we draw near to Him, He will draw near to us (James 4:8).

Beloved, you are seen, known, heard, and loved. And when we pray with those truths in mind, the atmosphere changes. Prayer helps us move from a place of distress to a place of rest.

God longs for us to reach out to Him—often. In 1 Thessalonians 5:17-18, the apostle Paul encourages us to "pray without ceasing; ...for this is God's will for you in Christ Jesus" (NASB). Notice Paul says "without ceasing." To clarify, this doesn't mean we quit our job, abandon our household duties, and lay prostrate on the floor 24/7. What Paul means here is that we commit to make prayer a regular habit—so much so that it becomes our lifeline, our go-to, when chaos ensues.

Prayer helps us move from a place of distress to a place of rest.

Does making prayer a regular habit help me not only in the area I'm praying about but also in other areas of my life? I truly believe so. Whenever and however we might pray, when we assume a posture of prayer (eyes closed, bowed head, on our knees, hands folded or raised to the sky), we acknowledge God's authority over us. When we pray, we welcome Him into our hearts, making space for His Spirit to move in us.

Jesus lived a life of prayer and encouraged his disciples to pray according to the Father's will: "And I will do whatever you ask in my name, so that the Father may be glorified in the Son" (John 14:13).

God is not a genie in a bottle that we rub when we want Him to grant our wishes; but if we pray according to His will and with the right heart motive, we can trust He will grant us what we truly desire, even if the answer to what we've asked is no or not yet. Yet I think that somewhere along the way in our faith journeys, many of us—myself included—write this off as too good to be true.

Say it with me: *Prayer is not too good to be true.* Prayer is the truest and surest thing we have in this life. And knowing and believing that our prayers matter and increase our faith changes everything. This is true for prayer about every aspect of life, not just prayer regarding decisions.

The enemy will tell us that our prayers don't matter. He would rather have us spin our wheels all day and night, working ourselves into a tailspin so that we are unable to make a decision based on faith rather than feelings. But God wants to speak to us and give us peace in our decisions. And the best way He can speak to us is through prayer—when we go to Him and ask Him to speak to us.

All it takes is one small step of faith to transform your prayer life. It doesn't matter if you're a new follower of Christ or have been a prayer warrior for years—God wants to take you deeper into faith through your prayers. He doesn't just want you to pray before bed out of habit. He wants you to pray as Paul described—without ceasing, out of a desire to be close to Him and hear from Him. He wants you to draw near, and through that nearness He wants to speak to you. He wants you to trust, know, and believe that He sees, hears, understands, and will answer when you call. He wants you to rely on Him to help you make both the tough and not-so-tough decisions of life.[2]

All that concerns you matters to God because *you* matter to God. Your faith matters to Him too; He wants to grow your faith, but it's a joint effort. The heart must yield to God before His hands can cultivate its soil. In this yielding, He wants to give you peace in your decisions, and the more you

When we have a pressing decision to make, it's not time to consult Google; it's time to get away with God.

exercise faith in this way, the more you will see how active and purposeful it is.

When we have a pressing decision to make, it's not time to consult Google; it's time to get away with God. Right then and there. Enter into prayer by thanking Him for the chance to be in relationship with Him. Then ask Him for insight and direction. If you're tired, scared, or confused, tell Him. He wants to hear every little detail. And unlike some friends, He never tires of listening. Ask Him to guide your thoughts and actions moving forward. Ask Him to bring you peace—the peace only He can give, the peace that reassures us we are following His will for us. When the time is right, He *will* direct your steps (Proverbs 16:9). And God is always on time!

Get Comfortable with Uncertainty

In addition to praying, another thing I've discovered that is important when making decisions by faith is accepting uncertainty. It's sort of like learning to let go of fear in the dark.

Darkness is something we fear. It's why kids take flashlights into the basement or their rooms at night. In many ways as adults, we still have the same basic fear: if we can't see a bright light, then we must be in the wrong place! In the miry black abyss, any shred of confidence or certainty is lost; only blindness, distrust, and confusion remain. What would seem tame (possible) in the light becomes wild and insufferable (impossible) in the face of darkness. But that's what darkness does. It clouds our judgment and keeps us from making decisions. In the dark we don't want to move one direction or the other because we don't know what might happen if we do.

The "darkness" I'm referring to may be a season when you don't see God moving or are unsure what is happening in your life. It literally feels like someone or something turned out the lights, disrupting the life you were living or the plans you were pursuing.

My own fear of literal darkness started at a young age when I became plagued by a series of recurring nightmares. Once or twice a week I dreamed that people were kidnapping me.

In the dream, I was home alone when I heard the sound of glass breaking downstairs. I quickly looked outside to see a bunch of burly men breaking into my house through the sunroom in the backyard. I tried to call 911, but it was too late. Before I finished telling the 911 operator my address, the men shoved a potato sack over my head and took me.

The dream always ended with me being thrown in the back of a semi—alone, afraid, and in complete darkness.

As an adult, I still don't like the darkness of feeling alone and unsure of where I am, but I'm learning to see that with God by my side, I don't have to fear what seems like darkness. This darkness often comes when I perceive a lack of response from God or I'm in a season of life marked by the loss of a loved one, sickness, or other distractions. But I can get through these times of darkness—and you can too—because God Himself is light; in Him there is no darkness (1 John 1:5). And though our feet may falter, His never will. He will bring us through every dark place or season when we ask Him to by faith.

Psalm 139:12 (NASB) is a great illustration of this. It is a verse that leaves me both awestruck and dumbfounded at the same time:

> Even the darkness is not dark to You,
> And the night is as bright as the day.
> Darkness and light are alike *to You.*

It strengthens my faith to know that darkness is not dark to God and the night is as bright as the day. While this is beyond my understanding, it is an overwhelming comfort whenever I find myself trying to walk through the darkness. We do not have to fear the darkness or the unknown because not only is our God not afraid of it, His very presence expels it. I believe this because I've felt it in my own heart and seen it with my own eyes—especially in regard to the people of my hometown of Elkhart, Indiana.

Growing up in the RV manufacturing capital of the world, I discovered quickly that almost every adult I knew worked for the RV industry in some capacity. If they weren't working inside the factory, then they might have been working in the corporate offices doing sales, marketing, customer service, or whatever other work they could to make ends meet. Or if they didn't work for an RV company, then they likely worked for a company that sold parts or services to the RV companies. You may be surprised to know that I've never actually ridden in an RV, although I did get ready in one for the Miss Elkhart County 4-H Fair Queen pageant back in high school. So, I guess that counts!

Faith directs and feeds us when we don't see what else will.

Everything was coming up roses for Elkhart, but darkness quickly descended on all of us when the Great Recession hit in 2008. Turns out, no one wants to buy an RV when the country is in a financial crisis. Looking back on it, I don't think there was a single person in Elkhart who didn't have a friend or family member who lost their job.

Things got so bad that a national news station sent reporters to live there and write stories about the financial crisis. They called it "The Elkhart Project." Months after the RV plants started to shut down, President Obama came to speak at my high school. Twice.

"The situation we face could not be more serious," Obama said. "…Economists from across the spectrum have warned that if we don't act immediately, millions of more jobs will be lost."[3]

His words made the darkness even more palpable, and I began to fear what all this would mean for my hometown. There wasn't a lot of faith in our government to help nor faith in our own decisions about what we would do if things went from bad to worse. Faith seemed to be across the room, or out of the room for many of us.

Days after the president's first speech, my dad called everyone into my grandparents' sunroom after our weekly Sunday family meal.

"I have some news to share with all of you," he said. "But first I want to play a song. It's called 'Even If,' and it's by Kutless."

The lyrics of this song are some of the most beautiful words in the world, and they have had a deep impact on my family. One of my favorite lines is:

> Even if the healing doesn't come…
> You are God, You are good.[4]

After three minutes and thirty-nine seconds of suspense, the song finally finished, and I looked across the room to see tears welling up in my dad's eyes.

"I've been let go," he said as he began to choke up. "But . . . I want you to know that I am not afraid. Yes, I've had this job for twelve and a half years, but I'm trusting God in this, and I know that even if things get bad, God will provide."

As the months went on and my dad struggled to find work, my parents' faith never faltered—or at least if it did, I certainly didn't see a shred of doubt. By faith, they continued to praise and honor God with the way they lived life and talked about my dad's job situation. They didn't hold anything back from God. In fact, they were bold and trusting enough to tithe from my dad's unemployment checks. Sounds totally crazy, right? If only you could have seen how God provided as a result of their trust and faithfulness.

To this day, remembering this experience strengthens my faith. In the face of overwhelming loss and uncertainty, my parents chose to put faith above fear, and that faith sustained them until deliverance came. Faith is like that: it directs and feeds us when we don't see what else will.

Making decisions by faith can feel a lot like navigating through the darkness. But if there's one thing I've learned about living by faith, it's that moving forward in the darkness comes with the territory. The prophet Isaiah described it this way: "And your ears shall hear a word behind you, saying, 'This is the way, walk in it,' when you turn to the right or when you turn to the left" (Isaiah 30:21 ESV). Here we see that faith requires journeying into the unknown. But we also see that when we allow ourselves to take a step into the unknown, God is faithful to let us know if we are on the right track.

The story of Joseph, Jesus's earthly father, and the decisions he made while walking with God is a wonderful example of this. I like the way Jon Bloom puts it in his book *Not by Sight*:

> One thing Joseph learned very quickly after God had drafted him to be the earthly father of Jesus was that his own plans were not a thing to be grasped. Whatever future he had originally imagined for himself and Mary evaporated in the heat of a reality determined by Another.
>
> And as he followed the path of faith, he repeatedly found it taking unpredictable turns: a Roman census, a grueling trip during the hardest part of pregnancy, a birth in a barn, no steady income, an assassination attempt, two desert crossings on foot with an infant, living in a foreign country, and waiting on God for last-minute guidance and

provision. This path was difficult, dangerous, expensive, time-consuming, and career delaying.

And it was all God's will.[5]

Like the detours in Joseph's chaotic journey, the twists and turns of our lives are not left to chance. I believe that God is sovereign and in control. And while we can't always understand what's happening, because His ways are not our ways (Isaiah 55:8-9), we aren't left on our own when it comes to making decisions that impact our right-now moments or our down-the-road moments. Where there is faith, there is a sure foundation for how we live life. God is our ultimate faith giver and our compass—a compass that is leading us to bigger, brighter, and better things than anything we can imagine.

Just think about what Joseph's life might have looked like before he chose to become the earthly father of Jesus. (After all, it was a *choice*. He could have told God no.) Maybe he had dreams of becoming Israel's greatest carpenter. Or maybe he wanted to get married and explore the world for a little while before settling down. We don't know what plans and desires Joseph stored in his heart, because those details are not written down for us. What we do know is that Joseph was a human being with real wants, needs, dreams, and plans; yet he willingly surrendered his life, including the decisions he made, to God.

Joseph recognized that navigating by faith sometimes means moving forward in the darkness. Even when he didn't understand when, where, why, or how the journey would unfold, He trusted God to lead and make a way where he couldn't see one, just as my parents did in the aftermath of the Great Recession.

There's a chance Joseph never received his dream job, dream house, or dream life; but because of his willingness to make his decisions by faith, he received something far greater: the gift of being Jesus's dad. Before he could do that, however, he had to get comfortable with making a move in the dark.

We first see that Joseph exercised faith in his decision-making in Matthew 1:18-25 when he came to accept the idea of Jesus as his son. We learn that while Joseph was pledged to be married to Mary, he also was a law-abiding citizen. So when he learned that Mary was expecting a child—perhaps she dropped by one day to tell him she was pregnant through the Holy Spirit—Joseph immediately decided to divorce her quietly to avoid any public shame (1:19).

Later that day, before Joseph acted on what he intended to do, an angel of the Lord appeared to him in a dream, telling him not to be afraid to take Mary as his wife. The angel went on to tell Joseph that the baby she was carrying was from the Holy Spirit and that they were to give him the name Jesus, because he was going to save his people from their sins (1:20-21).

Now, I don't know about you, but if an angel of the Lord came down to visit me, I'd listen to what the angel had to say; and that's exactly what Joseph did. Sure, he could have written the whole thing off as being a ridiculous claim, but he didn't. He listened to the angel and, by faith, did exactly as God had commanded him. God fulfilled the prophecy and promise of the birth of Jesus; and because Joseph had the courage to live by faith rather than divorce Mary, he had the blessed privilege of being Jesus's dad and experiencing all that came with raising a son, as well as seeing some part of the bigger mission that Jesus came to fulfill. When he acted on his faith, it brought fruit. And the same is true when we act on our faith.

When we read this story, there is a clear beginning and end. But for Joseph, nothing was certain about this story when it unfolded for him in real time. There was plenty of room for doubt and plenty of time to run away. Yet whatever doubts Joseph had, he was able to overcome them by faith and make a decision that ultimately would honor God's will and bring Him glory.

As my dear friend, mentor, and fellow author Barb Roose told me once:

In the decision-making process, we have to learn to embrace uncertainty. If our deepest desire is clarity (make my path clear or shut the wrong doors), then we may miss the faith journey God has planned for us. Some of the hardest decisions are the ones with three right answers or two great choices. In those cases, I've learned to stop obsessing over making the "right" decision and to trust God and apply wisdom and just make a decision. God isn't limited by our choices—sometimes we are, but He never is.[6]

Regardless of the uncertainties we face, we are promised that whether we turn to the left or to the right, God will be right behind us saying, "This is the way; walk in it" (Isaiah 30:21).

Make the Choice That Brings God Glory

Like Joseph, we face thousands of decisions every day, and the choices we make can either honor God or grieve His Spirit. This is why the apostle Paul urges us, "So whether you eat or drink or whatever you do, do it all for the glory of God" (1 Corinthians 10:31).

Jesus talks about how to do this in the parable of the three servants in Matthew 25, which He uses to illustrate the importance and impact of making faithful decisions, whether big or small. Before the servants' master leaves, he entrusts them with varying denominations of his hard-earned wealth. To one he gives five bags of gold, to another two bags, and to another one bag, each according to his ability (Matthew 25:15).

Fifteen years ago, if I'd received five bags of gold, I probably would have spent it all on candy, new clothes, and movie theater tickets with a side of jumbo popcorn. However, as an adult and the wife of a business owner, I've learned that money isn't everything—investment is. Before God called Alex to be a business owner, He blessed us with jobs that allowed us to save money for a down payment. We could have easily spent the money on more vacations, luxury dinners, and nicer cars and clothes, but instead we chose to be faithful to God's calling and invest for the future. Once we secured the down payment, we put the money to work. We wanted to show that we had faith in God for the small things He'd given us. And that's what I think Jesus's point is in the parable of the three servants—that when we are faithful in the big and small decisions of life, He will bless us with opportunities for more to give us an even greater capacity for faith.

The servants who received five or two bags of gold do not go out and spend it on frivolous things, but they also do not ignore the blessing. They invest the money wisely and double the amount of gold their master has given them (vv. 16-17). But the man who received one bag goes off, digs a hole in the ground, and hides the master's money (v. 18).

When the master returns, he is pleased with the servants who invested what he gave them. He says, "Well done, good and faithful servant! You have been faithful with a few things; I will put you in charge of many things. Come and share your master's happiness!" (vv. 21, 23). But when the master runs into the servant who hid his wealth out of fear, he is anything but pleased. There is no happiness in this exchange. Instead, the master rebukes the servant for his foolishness and fires him (vv. 24-30).

Faith is our compass in the deep.

God has given us the gift of free will. But as we see in this passage, misusing that gift to make selfish decisions can lead to unfortunate consequences. On the other hand, when we obey God and make decisions that bring Him glory, God blesses us with the eternal gifts of the Spirit: love, joy, peace, patience, kindness, goodness, faithfulness, gentleness, and self-control.

There are only two options when it comes to making decisions: we can be selfish with the opportunities God gives us, or we can be faithful and make choices that honor and glorify Him. We can say, "I'm doing this for me because it's what I want to do," or "God, this is what I'm faced with.... What would you have me do in this situation?" Whatever we choose, God's Word promises a sweet reward for those who remain faithful—a reward far greater than anything we could ever dream of: His very presence.

> My eyes will be on the faithful in the land,
>   that they may dwell with me;
> the one whose walk is blameless
>   will minister to me.
>
> No one who practices deceit
>   will dwell in my house;
> no one who speaks falsely
>   will stand in my presence.
>
> (Psalm 101:6-7)

Making decisions by faith frees us from making wrong decisions because it helps us choose things that align with God's Word and will for our lives. Having God's peace and presence also frees us from the doubt, guilt, and uncertainty that sometimes accompany making decisions in the darkness. Most importantly, it allows us to push past our selfish agendas and the noise of this world to live as God desires us to live.

Living by faith isn't living blindly at all; in fact, engaging our faith in the decision-making process gives us the clearest vision we will ever have. Faith is our compass in the deep.

GOING DEEPER

1. Do you tend to be a decisive or indecisive person? How might prayer positively impact your decision-making process?

2. Imagine that a friend comes to you with a situation and doesn't know what decision to make. Based on what we've learned in this chapter, what would you encourage your friend to do?

3. Read Proverbs 3:5-6 and Proverbs 12:15. How would you describe the difference between these two types of decision makers?

PRAYER

Father God, thank You for the gift of life. Thank You for the many blessings You have poured on me, including free will and the ability to make decisions. Thank You for letting me have choices. I am not a robot who is being forced to do things. I am a person with a beating heart, an active mind, and a free spirit. Help me learn how to make decisions by faith, even when the road ahead is unclear. Help me not to fear the darkness but to look to You and trust You with every move I make. I want to honor and glorify You in my decisions, but I know I can't always do that on my own. I need Your help. So, transform my selfish, pride-filled heart into a faithful, servant's heart. Let every choice I make bring You praise. In Jesus's name. Amen.

CHAPTER TEN

Living with a Victory Mindset

For everyone born of God is victorious and overcomes the world; and this is the victory that has conquered and overcome the world—our [continuing, persistent] faith [in Jesus the Son of God].

—*1 John 5:4 AMP*

A few years ago, Alex and I had the opportunity to see Michael Phelps swim his last race on American soil at the 2016 Olympic Trials in Omaha. You would think that since I met Michael at a University of Michigan swim camp when I was thirteen, my star-struck emotions would be diminished. Not a chance. Goosebumps lined my arms and legs as we pulled up to the CenturyLink Center, which boasted a larger-than-life-sized banner of Michael celebrating in victory over a past Olympic win.

After waiting in line for thirty minutes, we finally made it to section

224, seats 9 and 10. I don't eat a lot of candy anymore (except dark choco-late, of course), but I sure felt like a kid in a candy store as I leaned over the railing to get a closer look at the action happening on deck. I inhaled the chlorine-scented environment and an inerasable smile spread across my face. These were my people. This was my sport. And I was about to watch history being made. Cue the giddy schoolgirl squeals.

Amid the flurry of activity, Michael appeared from the athlete holding area wearing a camouflage zip up, white Beats, and his signature MP suit, swim cap, and goggles.

"This is the championship finals for the men's 100-meter butterfly," the announcer declared.

Seven short and one long whistle blow summoned the swimmers to step onto the starting blocks, where Michael performed his famous pre-race arm swings in lane seven.

"Take your mark," the official said, and with one beep from the start-ing system, the eight swimmers were off. But Michael was not in first place off the blocks or going into the turn.

Because I saw the race go down in real time, I didn't hear the tele-vision announcer's commentary until I watched the footage the next day to relive the experience. Their predictions and exclamations catalog the exact thoughts running through my head during the fifty-one seconds of Michael's swim.

"There's no doubt he will not be first going into this wall," one said at the fifty-meter turn.

They were right. Michael touched the wall in fourth place before turning to bring it home. With less than half the race left to go, shouts and screams escalated from all around the arena. If there was a noise-o-meter on the premises, the gauge would have been in the red zone, right at the top.

And then, with less than fifteen meters to go, Michael turned on the heat, kicking with every ounce of energy he had left.

"He might win it..." The announcer paused to wait and see the final results. "He did it! Once again Phelps proves that when it's all on the line, he's got something special."

One month later in Rio, Michael became the most decorated Olympian of all time and the only US Olympian to win four consecutive gold medal titles in a single event. When the closing ceremonies called Michael's competitive career into completion, the swimmer had twenty-three gold, three silver and two bronze medals to commemorate his many victories.

Victory, sweet victory.

I still remember my first taste of it when I qualified for the Indiana Age Group State Championships in the fifty- and hundred-yard freestyle and butterfly. The victory of simply being on deck at the famous IU Natatorium was sweeter than Southern iced tea with a side of pecan pie.

What about you? Can you recall a time when you experienced victory in your own life? Maybe you landed the dream job you thought you could never achieve. Maybe you crushed a sporting record. Maybe you became a parent. Maybe you mastered an instrument you always wanted to learn how to play.

What did the victory taste like? How did it feel? Did you jump for joy, sing a song, smile, dance, or pump your fists in the air?

Meeting goals and seizing victories in life feel amazing. But the victory we have in Christ, who conquered death for our salvation—well, that victory is more amazing than anything we can imagine. And when we learn to live with that victory always in the back of our minds, we will finally experience the mindset of victory that God longs for us to have.

Trading Mindsets

"I think I can, I think I can, I think I can." Many of us are familiar with the story of *The Little Engine That Could*, where one small engine's tenacity allows it to overcome the seemingly impossible task of pulling a train over a steep mountain.

While "I think I can" is an honorable mindset to adopt, there's a better mindset for us to grab on to as sons and daughters of the Reigning King—one that takes the pressure off our efforts and abilities and puts it onto the One who is responsible for our victory in the first place.

The mindset is still four words, but instead of "I think I can" it's "I know He will, I know He will, I know He will."

Beloved, I cannot even begin to tell you what adopting this mindset has done for me. You'll recall that in the first chapter of this book I said that at one point in my life the only thing I had faith in was my certainty of drowning—of losing the fight. I had adopted a defeated mindset, and it was devouring me from the inside out. If I were Michael Phelps coming in fourth at the turn, I would have sighed and let myself believe there was no chance of winning.

In the Book of Exodus, we find that this is how the Israelites initially felt when God released them from Egyptian slavery and began to lead them on a journey to the Promised Land. The journey should have been full of joy and great expectation, but instead the Israelites gave in to defeat when things didn't go the way they had hoped or planned. Instead of spending their days trusting God for victory, they grumbled, complained, and moaned around the desert. As a result, a trip that should have taken eleven days took forty years.

After wandering through the wilderness for nearly half a century, a new generation of Israelites was raised up to do what their ancestors could not: enter the Promised Land. But before they could cross the Jordan and conquer Jericho, God prepared His people by teaching them about what it means to have a courageous faith—a faith that trades a defeated mindset for one of victory. Through Joshua, God commanded His people: "'Be strong and courageous. Do not be afraid; do not be discouraged, for the LORD your God will be with you wherever you go'" (Joshua 1:9).

With God on our side, there is nothing we can't do. But without Him we are like the Israelites who wandered in the wilderness for forty years: hopeless and powerless—the opposite of courageous. We are cowards, prone to despair, self-preservation, and timidity.

Left to our own devices, we cannot guarantee victory, but He can. And He already has. This is the good news of the gospel! Jesus has already conquered death and overcome the grave to give us victory in Him. Hallelujah, what a Savior!

Faith in Jesus is our ticket to victory.

Because of Jesus, victory is our birthright, and we can claim it proudly. As John so beautifully puts in 1 John 5:4 (AMP): "For everyone born of God is victorious *and* overcomes the world; and this is the victory that has conquered *and* overcome the world—our [continuing, persistent] faith [in Jesus the Son of God]."

It's simple: faith in Jesus is our ticket to victory.

While we might only see things one battle at a time, God sees the bigger picture; and when all is said and done, we won't have to guess who will win because the war has already been won. Give God your defeated mindset and watch as He fortifies you with the strength and courage you need to overcome and claim the victory that's rightfully yours. And there is great joy in victory!

All About That Joy

I don't think I've ever watched a Super Bowl or Stanley Cup game where the winning team didn't overflow with joy and storm the field or ice rink when the clock ran out. It's no wonder, because when you're on the winning team, everything you've trained for, everything you've fought for, and everything you've believed in becomes true and worth it. Beloved, with God on your side, you are on the winning team!

Being on the winning team means that every minute you spend

praying and reading God's Word, every day you chase hard after God and follow His leading, every time you suit up and make God-honoring decisions, every time you choose faith over fear, every time you trust God's promises over your problems—it's all worth it. Because in the end, we win. This life is only the beginning, and it's nothing compared to the eternity we get to spend with Jesus in the wonder of heaven.

Your sins and mistakes don't have the last word. Your anxiety, depression, terminal or chronic illness, broken relationships, government, finances, and past, present, or future experiences can't take this victory away from you either. If knowing this doesn't bring a smile to your face, I don't know what will!

When doctors diagnosed me with hEDS, their verdict signaled a new chapter for me, one I so desperately wanted to approach with courage and faith. But the enemy of my soul had other plans. Let's call it "Operation Steal Lauren's Joy."

Like faith and victory, joy is a gift from the Father, and all three are connected. Faith gives us victory, and victory brings us joy. So, what happens when it feels like our victory has been snatched? Hasta la vista joy, baby.

In the months following my diagnosis, the enemy threw all the fiery arrows he could at me to try and hijack my joy. He wanted me to believe victory was impossible for a genetically flawed woman like me. My pain quickly grew to intolerable levels. The throbbing, aching, and stabbing sensations were so excruciating that I sobbed in agony every day on my way home from my stressful, full-time job. My jaw degenerated to the point where I couldn't sing, talk, or eat without it hurting. Though I'd sung on a worship team since high school, the pain forced me to quit. Not long after stepping down from the stage, my digestive system fell into disarray and my anxiety pushed me to the edge of having another breakdown.

Let me tell you how tempting it was to give in to bitterness during this time. I felt like Naomi of the Old Testament did after losing it all and blaming God for making her life unpleasant. Scripture tells us she actually changed her name from Naomi, meaning "my joy" and "pleasant one," to Mara, or "bitter one," to express the pain she harbored (Ruth 1:20). Fortunately, God is always working for the good of those who love Him, and He redeemed Naomi's story (Ruth 4) just as He's been redeeming mine over the years.

You might be surprised to know that as the founder of She Found Joy, I haven't always been so joyful. When life gave me lemons, I didn't make lemonade. Instead, I let the acid penetrate and poison my heart, and with that poisoning came a slow and silent hardening of my heart. It's not like I woke up one morning and instantly felt cold, sad, and bitter toward the world. I didn't *want* my heart to become hard; it just happened.

The more I dwelled on the mess of my life instead of the victory of the cross, the harder my heart became—and the harder it was to find joy in the everyday.

I wonder if you've ever felt the same way.

Maybe you've lost a loved one and you never had the chance to say goodbye. Maybe your company did its annual round of layoffs and your job got cut. Maybe the husband you once fell in love with has become someone you no longer know. Maybe you're single and wondering if God will ever send that special someone into your life. Maybe you don't know if you'll have enough money to get your kids Christmas presents this year. Or maybe, like me, you've been given a diagnosis you never wanted to receive and you're thinking, *I don't have anything to be joyful about, Lauren!*

I understand. I've been through some of those deep waters too. I still have days when I don't want to get out of bed. I cry. I pray for God to heal me and take all the pain away. But let me tell you what I've learned: Amid all the suffering and chaos, we still have a choice, and that choice is whether we will abide in bitterness or abide in the joy of the Lord. Living joyfully doesn't mean we will always be happy; it means that our outlook can be hopeful and joyful in the deep, painful seasons of life.

Beloved, it's time we reclaim the victory mindset. It's time we get our joy back and delight in it daily. Do not let the enemy steal your joy, for as Nehemiah so poignantly reminds us: "'The joy of the LORD is your strength'" (Nehemiah 8:10).

> *Living joyfully doesn't mean we will always be happy; it means that our outlook can be hopeful and joyful in the deep, painful seasons of life.*

There's a reason I commissioned a talented hand-lettering artist I know to create a print of this verse for my office. Victory is our birthright, but joy? Joy is what allows us to thrive in the deep waters of life. When we know, believe, and follow Jesus, the Holy Spirit produces great joy in our hearts, and that joy becomes our strength to carry on because we know how the story ends. In the end, we win. And living from that place of joy gives us strength because we are living with a victory mindset.

Singer-songwriter Meghan Trainor may be "all about that bass, 'bout that bass, no treble."[1] But me? Regardless of my circumstances, I'm all about that joy, 'bout that joy, no trouble. What do you want to be about?

GOING DEEPER

1. Can you remember a time when you experienced a victory in your life? How did that victory make you feel?
2. In what areas of your life do you feel defeated? What's one step you can take toward claiming the victory of Christ over your circumstances?

3. Read 1 Peter 1:8-9 and Hebrews 12:2. How does your definition of joy today compare to the definition found in these Scriptures?

4. Imagine yourself living each day out of the victory and joy that come from Jesus's victory. How would that kind of life impact the battles you face? What's keeping you from claiming victory and joy in the deep?

PRAYER

Heavenly Father, I come to You today so in need of Your presence. So in need of Your joy. God, this life can be so hard. The road can be so weary, and my soul can grow faint. But Your love is stronger. You've given me victory over the grave, and when I am downcast and defeated, You promise to fill me with a joy that allows me to be strong and carry on. Give me a deeper understanding of joy today, Lord. Help me learn to receive and live out of the victory and joy You have so freely given me. No matter what comes my way, help me dance for joy when I remember what You've done for me. Thank You for your Word, Lord, and for how good You are to me. Thank You for sending Your Son to bring victory and joy to the world. In Jesus's name. Amen.

CHAPTER ELEVEN

Sharing Faith

Our faith becomes stronger as we express it;
a growing faith is a sharing faith.

—Billy Graham[1]

W hen I was in college, I worked the weekend morning shift as Salty Tart Bakery's front-of-the-house server and cashier in downtown Minneapolis. The owner, renowned pastry chef Michelle Gayer, was the recipient of two James Beard Award nominations; and as an amateur baker, I marveled at the thought of working under such talent.

My roommates probably thought I was crazy waking up at 3:45 a.m. for work, but once I'd rubbed the sleep from my eyes and torched my first crème brûlée of the day, the time didn't faze me. When you're living the dream, you don't care about silly things like sleep. And helping serve the people of Minneapolis their fill of creamy coconut macaroons, decadent cookies, cupcakes, pastry-cream-filled brioche, savory puff pastries, and fragrant French bread made losing a few hours of shut-eye worth it.

As a girl who grew up baking cookies with her mom on the regular, one of my favorite perks of the job was watching the head bakers whip up a batch of peanut butter, chocolate cherry, or triple chocolate chip cookies. I watched in wonder as they rolled out the dough and stamped it with circle cookie cutters to make perfectly thick, round shapes. After they cut the dough, I got to help transfer the uncooked circles onto a baking sheet to chill in the commercial fridge before being baked the next morning.

It took every ounce of self-control I had not to devour every single one of those cookies before putting them out for customers. I considered it my lucky day when a dab of gooey chocolate landed on my finger as I stacked the display trays. One taste of chocolate does a body, mind, and soul good. Amen?

Though my love for chocolate will never fade, the faith I've found in Jesus is sweeter and more satisfying than any cookie could ever be. And yet, how many of us are content to keep our faith to ourselves, away from the world and impossible for others to discover and enjoy in the same way we have?

As we read in chapter 9, we are called to bring glory to God—whether we eat or drink or whatever we do (1 Corinthians 10:31). While there are plenty of definitions out there for what it means to glorify God, Beth Moore says it well: "We glorify God to the degree that we externalize the internal presence of the living Christ."[2] In other words, we glorify God when we live out of the presence of Christ who lives within us.

Sharing and living out our faith brings glory to God, because we are pointing others to the hope of Jesus. But keeping our faith to ourselves? Well, that's like refusing to share a batch of freshly baked chocolate chip cookies!

Here's another analogy for you: Not living out our faith is like holding a fire extinguisher in our hands and neglecting to use it while the whole world is burning around us. We have the solution to the fire, but we choose not to do anything about it.

Why, then, do so many of us practice our faith in quiet isolation rather than share it? I posed this question to my followers on social media, and here are some of the responses I received:

- I assume they already know about Jesus because I live in the Bible Belt.
- I'm afraid of failing—disappointing God or others.
- I feel like I'm not good enough. I don't feel qualified to share when I'm so imperfect.
- I am worried what others will think about me if I live out my faith.
- It feels like there's not enough time in the day between work and school.
- I am a people pleaser, and so I keep things to myself. Don't want to step on toes.

Can you identify with any of these responses? I admit that in the beginning stages of ministry, I feared what others would think about me when I started to live out my faith in Jesus. For years I had practiced faith in isolation. But when I discovered a deep, saving faith—the kind we've been discussing in this book—I realized I couldn't afford not to live it out. The stakes were too high. People all around me were drowning, and I had the Lifesaver they needed: Jesus!

The world needs your faith today now more than ever.

It's up to us to be the light of Christ in this dark world. We cannot afford to keep our faith to ourselves. We have to live it out.

Made for More

In the Book of Esther, we meet a woman who wasn't afraid to live out her faith in order to make a difference for the kingdom of God. In a moment of history when the lives of the entire Jewish population were on the line, Esther could have shrunk back in fear; but instead she stepped up to save God's people.

Now, before I share Esther's shining moment, which we find in chapter 4, let me give you some of the backstory. We are first introduced to Esther, the cousin of Mordecai, in Esther 2:7. At that time, King Xerxes was searching for a new queen; and without knowing she was a Jew, he set his sights on Esther. Meanwhile, Mordecai, who had adopted Esther after her parents died, stayed close to her by becoming a government official. After King Xerxes made Esther his queen, Mordecai found himself in conflict with the king's second-in-command, Haman. Although he was happy to serve the king, Mordecai refused to bow down to Haman when ordered. Needless to say, Haman was outraged by Mordecai's behavior; and after finding out that he was a Jew, Haman ordered that all the Jews be killed.

Not long after the king's declaration, Hathak, one of Esther's eunuchs, went to speak with a very distressed Mordecai. After giving Hathak a copy of Haman's death sentence for the Jews, Mordecai instructed the eunuch to show it to Esther, who could beg for mercy and plead with Xerxes for her people's lives.

Esther was hesitant to heed Mordecai's advice, and rightfully so. This was a time when, according to Persian law, anyone who approached the king without being summoned would be put to death. I don't know about you, but if something's going to hurt or kill me, I'm probably not going to do that thing out of fear. And I think that's where a lot of us are today in an age when so many do not have faith. God has called us to live out our faith in the world, but so often we ignore the call. We don't speak up. We don't have the courage to make a difference for the Kingdom. Because we're afraid.

Perhaps today we can glean some courage from what happens next in Esther's story:

> When Esther's words were reported to Mordecai, he sent back this answer: "Do not think that because you are in the king's house you alone of all the Jews will escape. For if you remain silent at this time, relief and deliverance for the Jews will arise from another place, but you and your father's family will perish. And who knows but that you have come to your royal position for such a time as this?"
>
> Then Esther sent this reply to Mordecai: "Go, gather together all the Jews who are in Susa, and fast for me. Do not eat or drink for three days, night or day. I and my attendants will fast as you do. When this is done, I will go to the king, even though it is against the law. And if I perish, I perish." (Esther 4:12-16)

This passage of Scripture amazes me. Think about it: Esther was the queen. She could have lived an easy life, filled with expensive jewelry, lavish clothing, and delicious food. She didn't have to do anything. And yet she wasn't overcome by fear but chose to be used by God—even if her obedience led to death. She knew the law, but she also knew her God.

He was the God who saved Noah's family from destruction. The God who delivered the children of Israel from slavery in Egypt. The God who gave Joshua the courage needed to lead the Israelites after Moses's death. Esther knew this same God, and she knew He could be trusted because of His great faithfulness.

So here we see that even though darkness was descending upon the people of Israel, there was still hope—hope that Esther would have faith, take courage in the Lord, and glorify Him by putting her faith into action and saving her people.

In her willingness to be used by God, Esther ended up saving an entire nation. She knew the risks were great, but she also knew that her God was greater. So instead of choosing fear, she chose faith. Though she may have had some fear—after all, she was human—she overcame that fear by choosing to be courageous and allowing her faith to bring great glory to God.

I look up to Esther for many reasons, but I especially admire her ability to choose faith over fear. We might not be the queen of Persia, but beloved, this is a decision you and I have to make every day too.

Fear taunts us and says, "Don't talk about Jesus. It's too risky. You don't know what will happen if you speak up. People might laugh at you or turn against you. It's not worth it. After all, you're just one person anyway, so what difference would you make? Keep your faith to yourself."

Fear taunts us and pushes us back, but faith says, "Press on, beloved. God is with you, God is for you, and God has gone before you. You can trust Him. Keep swimming." With every step we take, faith propels us forward, encouraging and guiding us along the way. Faith commands us to push fear aside and step into the role we were created for—the role of being not only a child of God but also a change maker for the Kingdom.

Shine His Light

We've talked a lot about how to cultivate a courageous faith that can survive the deep waters of life's journey. But while it's good to know these things, this new knowledge and perspective mean nothing if we do not apply them to our purpose.

We have one beautiful life to live, and during this lifetime Jesus calls us to do more than just grow in our own personal faith. Before He ascended into heaven, Jesus commanded us to "go and make disciples" (Matthew 28:19). This is the Great Commission—to spread His light and make His name known. But it's up to us to take this command to heart. It's up to us to answer the call God has placed on our lives.

My favorite thing about the Great Commission is that there is no cookie-cutter way to shine for Jesus. Each of us has been given a unique role and talents for the cause of Christ. That means we don't have to compare our role to somebody else's role, because we've all been given a different mission as part of the larger mission of sharing the good news of Christ.

You may be thinking: I'm just one person, Lauren. What difference could I possibly make?

> There is no cookie-cutter way to shine for Jesus.

The truth is, you're already making a difference just by desiring a deeper experience of God and a life of courageous faith, evidenced by the fact that you are reading this book. And when we come to the last page together, we can continue to make a difference by the way we choose to live our lives.

Whether we like to acknowledge it or not, as we go about our days, people are watching our every move. When we choose to live courageous, bold, loving, joyful, sacrificial, and faith-filled lives, we make an incredible difference by being an example for others and a conduit of God's grace. But it doesn't stop there. You see, being the light of the world, as Jesus described in Matthew 5:14-16, isn't about being a good person; it's about loving others because God first loved us. It's about taking time to interact with people and cultivate relationships. It's about being like Esther and stepping out in faith. It's about realizing that perhaps we were born for such a time as this—to be the light and make a difference.

God might not call you to be a queen and sacrifice your life for an entire nation, but He will call you to something.

I remember that when I first felt God calling me into women's ministry, I laughed. I let fear make my decisions for me. Who, me? Certainly not me, God. I know you already have plenty of women filling those shoes. It's too much work. There are so many others who have more experience or credentials. What difference could I possibly make?

I don't know what God will call me to next, but what I do know is this: I don't have to know all the details; I just have to keep the faith and be courageous enough to share it with others. And the same is true for you.

One of the verses I'm clinging to these days is Philippians 4:19 (NASB), and I encourage you to memorize this verse and recall it as you're swimming through uncharted waters: "And my God will supply all your needs according to His riches in glory in Christ Jesus."

No one and no thing is a match for our God.

This verse is a constant reminder that though I may not feel like I have what it takes to be the hands and feet of Jesus, God does. And because He promises to supply every need, I don't have to worry about what I lack. All I have to do is keep shining the light of Jesus and sharing the faith and hope I've found in Him. I have found that when I do, God takes care of the rest.

The road has been bumpy and I've made a lot of mistakes since stepping into ministry. I've said yes to things I shouldn't have said yes to. I've strayed off the path. I've been afraid of failure and have been rejected more times than I can count. But I've also discovered what it feels like to be caught in the rhythms of God's grace. Because here's what I've realized after saying yes to courageous faith: no matter how far I stray, as long as I keep living for God and choose faith over fear, He is faithful to get me through anything I face.

And you know what? He'll be faithful to do the same for you.

The same God who protected, defended, and strengthened Esther is the same God who is protecting, defending, and strengthening us today.

The apostle Paul says in Romans 8:28-31:

And we know that in all things God works for the good of those who love him, who have been called according to his purpose. For those God foreknew he also predestined to be conformed to the image of his Son, that he might be the firstborn among many brothers and sisters. And those he predestined, he also called; those he called, he also justified; those he justified, he also glorified.

What, then, shall we say in response to these things? If God is for us, who can be against us?

No one and no thing is a match for our God. So you know what, friend? We don't have to fear answering the call to shine brightly for Jesus. We can trust that the God who keeps us from drowning will guide us and give us the courage we need to be His light, even when we don't know what's ahead. And as we journey together with Him, His light will shine through our cracks to bring hope to a hopeless world.

GOING DEEPER

1. What keeps you from sharing your faith and shining God's light?
2. Reread Romans 8:28-31 and filter your answers to the first question through this passage of Scripture. How does this change your perspective on being God's light and bringing hope to the world?
3. What is one way you can show the love of Jesus to the world this week?

PRAYER

Father, I come before You as a child who is ready to do Your will and shine brightly for You. But sometimes it's hard to know exactly what that looks like, and so I ask that You would take my hand and lead me into Your will. Guide my steps and show me the way to go. Take away my fear, hesitation, sin, and shame, and give me Your courage, strength, and peace. Make my purpose so clear that there can be no denying what You've called me to do.

I want to love You and others as You love me, Jesus. I don't want to settle for having puppy love. I want to have a passionate, sacrificial love. Set my heart on fire to burn for You so that I may be your hands and feet in this broken world. When I wake up, give me the desire to live out the faith I've found in You. As I go about my day, give me the perspective I need to live intentionally for You. I pray against the spirit of isolation, Lord Jesus. For I know You made me to live in community. Let my faith cause others to have faith in You. In Jesus's name. Amen.

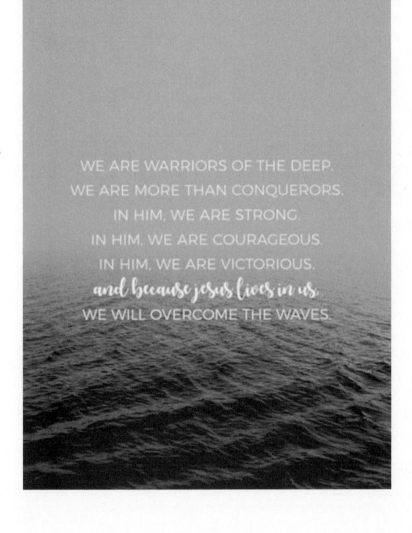

WE ARE WARRIORS OF THE DEEP.
WE ARE MORE THAN CONQUERORS.
IN HIM, WE ARE STRONG.
IN HIM, WE ARE COURAGEOUS.
IN HIM, WE ARE VICTORIOUS.
and because jesus lives in us,
WE WILL OVERCOME THE WAVES.

CHAPTER TWELVE

Warrior of the Deep

*Christian faith does not offer us a peaceful way to come to terms with death.
No, it offers instead a way to overcome death.*

—*Philip Yancey*[1]

Five fishermen set out on a shark-fishing expedition from Mexico's Pacific Coast fishing village of San Blas. The crew expected the trip to last a few days, but when a cold front and strong wind dragged their twenty-five-foot boat out to sea, they found themselves adrift without gas, food, or water.

With no shelter or sustenance on board, the men hid under blankets to protect themselves from the sun, and they crafted fishing rods from broken engine parts. When fish, ducks, and sharks were in short supply, they caught seagulls and ate them raw. Knowing saltwater could not quench their thirst, they waited patiently for rain and collected the precipitation in buckets to survive.

Although the fishermen lacked material comforts, one possession managed to survive the wear and tear of the journey: a tattered Bible, which they took turns reading from as they continuously prayed for God to rescue them. But as the days and weeks turned into four months, only three remained: Jesus Vidana, Salvador Ordonez, and Lucio Rendon.

By this time, most of the town of San Blas had given them up for dead. But Vidana's mother refused to lose hope, and the fishermen were equally determined to fight for faith and keep hope alive.

Then, after nine months of drifting, a Taiwanese trawler found the crew—naked, burned, and emaciated—near the Marshall Islands, more than five thousand miles from San Blas.

Upon their rescue, Vidana told news reporters, "We never lost hope because there is a God up there."[2]

When all hope seemed lost, these men chose courage and faith over fear and doubt, making prayer the source of their strength. And when they were finally rescued, they returned home warriors. Each one was a warrior of the deep.

That's what you and I are: warriors of the deep. We are each a courageous fighter, engaged and experienced in deep-water warfare, struggles, and conflicts. And it's not just who we are—it's who God is:

> "The LORD is a warrior;
> the LORD is his name." (Exodus 15:3)

Our Father is the mightiest warrior of all!

What do you do as a warrior in the deep? You keep believing against all hope just as Abraham, the father of faith, did (Romans 4:18). Like the five fishermen lost at sea, you are strengthened when you surrender your life to God and put your faith in Him, who gives you the courage to overcome. This is what we've been exploring in this book. And before our journey comes to a close, I want to introduce you to a few warriors who have, by God's grace, learned to survive and thrive in the deep. When the waves threatened to take them out or they felt lost at sea, they did not lose faith. Instead, they swam deeper into God's presence and love, building endurance in Him and claiming victory over their circumstances.

I pray that this final chapter and these stories can encourage you to keep fighting the good fight of faith when you'd rather give in to the waves. When you are tempted to despair, I pray you will pull out this book and flip to this chapter to be reminded of the simple fact that hope is never lost. (Then flip to chapter 8, where you'll find The Faithful Swimmer's Battle Plan.)

Remember the promises of Isaiah 61:1-4, which we know are fulfilled in Jesus: He will bring good news to your affliction. He will bind up your broken heart. He will fill your soul with freedom and use His light to eclipse whatever darkness tries to ensnare you. He will comfort you in your mourning. On your head, He will bestow a crown of beauty instead of ashes. He will anoint you with the oil of joy instead of mourning and clothe you with a garment of praise instead of a spirit of despair. He will rebuild and restore what has been broken and ruined. He will. He will. He will. Because that's exactly what He was sent here to do (Luke 4:14-21).

This is the hope we all must choose to hold on to, even when the odds are stacked against us. So meet my dear friends and fellow warriors of the deep, and be inspired by their stories of unrelenting hope and courageous faith.

Ready for Anything: Heather Dixon

Heather Dixon was sitting on her screened-in porch listening to the early morning songs of backyard birds when God told her to get ready.

Wanting to confirm what she had heard with God's Word, she picked up her Bible to find the first time these two words appeared in Scripture. Her search led her to Joshua 1:2: "Moses my servant is dead. Now then, you and all these people, get ready to cross the Jordan River into the land I am about to give to them—to the Israelites."

As she dove into God's Word to learn more about getting ready, her gut told her something was coming. She just didn't know what.

Over the next five months, Heather suffered a miscarriage, a partial kidney infarction, two aneurysms, and a ruptured carotid artery. Soon after, she was diagnosed with Vascular Ehlers-Danlos Syndrome (vEDS), a genetic connective tissue disorder that makes blood vessels, arteries, and organs prone to spontaneous rupture. There is no cure or treatment for it, only a prescription from the doctor to prepare your bucket list and live your life well. The average life expectancy of someone with vEDS is forty-eight years.

God's light and love allow us to be ready for whatever unknowns the deep waters bring.

I first met Heather a little less than a year after we both were diagnosed with different forms of Ehlers-Danlos Syndrome (EDS)—hypermobile for me, vascular for her. To say our meeting was anything less than the ridiculously gracious and generous hand of God would be a complete disservice. In a season of my life when I thought I might sink beneath the waves once more, God gave me Heather to remind me to take courage, have faith, and fix my gaze on Jesus, not on the seas that raged around me.

Never have I ever met a woman more courageous and steadfast than Heather. God has used her in many ways to propel me in my faith journey, and I am forever grateful for the chance to know her and do ministry together.

Today Heather is one of my best friends and a treasured ministry partner, but more than that, she is one of the fiercest warriors of the deep I know. Why? Because she is ready.

She has taken to heart God's instruction to Joshua to be strong and courageous. No matter what the day brings, Heather refuses to let fear or anxiety have a foothold in her life. Instead she lives with hope and purpose, understanding that every moment truly is a gift from God.

If you know Heather or follow her online, you know she's a big proponent of bucket-list living. Not the travel-around-the-world-and-go-sky-diving type of bucket-list living (although she'd never turn down a trip to Disney World), but the kind of living that makes choices in the moment and cherishes the details along the way.

Heather is as fierce and faithful as they come, not because of who she is but because of God's faithfulness and redeeming love. She writes:

> True to His gracious nature, God has taken one of our hardest seasons of life and turned it into one of the sweetest. Every moment is precious. Every memory is priceless. For every day that we are given, my family and I are thankful. Because of God's love, I now have what many people spend their entire lives searching for: gratitude for both the mundane and the miracle, and hope in a Savior who can redeem all things. Even the darkest of stories are no match for God's light.[3]

Heather is a living testimony that God's light and love allow us to be ready for whatever unknowns the deep waters bring. And even in the midst of a battle, we can love because God first loved us. We can have faith because our God is faithful, and we can be fierce because our heavenly Father is as fierce as they come.

With Jesus, we can be ready for anything. And when we put our faith in Him, we will win in the end because He always wins.

Mercy and Life After Loss: Lisa Appelo

Lisa met her future husband, Dan, in seventh grade when their families started attending the same church. Though they started out as just friends, after logging in many church trips, choir practices, and surf outings together, Dan asked Lisa out around her sixteenth birthday.

Dan may have been Lisa's first boyfriend, but as she got ready for their first real date, she sensed it was the start of the rest of their life together. Dan wasn't like your typical high-school teenager. He brought flowers to every single date he and Lisa went on. He was confident without being arrogant, adventurous without being dangerous, affectionate without being pushy—the kind of guy a girl could really see herself growing old with.

On their second date, Dan and Lisa went to a rural restaurant on Cross Creek, an old pocket of Florida made famous in Marjorie Kinnan Rawlings's Pulitzer Prize–winning book *The Yearling*. And as they shared their hopes and dreams with each other over fried alligator, cooter, and key lime pie, Lisa fell in love.

After twenty-six years of marriage and seven kids, Lisa and Dan's life together was sweet and full. Dan had landed his dream job, and opportunities were looking up. Lisa was deeply satisfied in parenting and homeschooling. Everything was fine. Until suddenly it wasn't.

Life as Lisa knew it shattered one day in the dark, early morning hours when heavy breathing from Dan's side of the bed woke her. At first she thought he was having a nightmare, so she nudged him and reassured him that everything was going to be OK. But when the labored breathing continued, Lisa realized her husband was not having a nightmare; he was having a heart attack.

After her son called 911, the operator walked Lisa through two rounds of CPR before asking her to stop and take a pulse. She couldn't find one but pressed on, hoping it was just her lack of skill. Within minutes, the paramedics arrived and transported Dan to the nearest hospital. But it was too late. Dan could not be revived.

"I felt like someone had suddenly ripped off one entire side of my body and left me with raw, dangling threads," Lisa writes on her blog. "Our life— tomorrow's plans, next week's list, our comfortable routine with the seven children we were raising—was shattered and would never be the same again. My four-year-old would grow up without her daddy. What about my littlest boy who would have no more Saturday trips to the hardware store or rides to the rental house in Dad's truck? I hated that my kids' lives were split wide open with such gut-wrenching grief."

After the ambulance left their house, Lisa had cried out for mercy. But God had not spared Dan. So there she was, a widow and single mom with a big choice to make: give in to grief and despair, or press on and trust that even in death, God is true and faithful.

Lisa will be the first to tell you that navigating these deep waters has not been easy, but as she has continued to choose to press into God, He has helped her get through every trial and every season since Dan's death. Lisa writes:

> [Here] is the mercy: That God continues to give us life in the suffer-
> ing. One doesn't stop for the other. Moments of joy intersect afflic-
> tion. It's not sequential or linear. But woven into the days of despair
> for what is no more and what will never be again, God is and His hope
> resuscitates. As the paramedics worked on Dan, I could utter only one
> prayer. "Have mercy on us, God. O God, have mercy on us." Till my
> dying day, I will shout from the rooftops that God is Faithful and True.
> He has been merciful.[4]

Seven years after that tragic morning, everything is not perfect. There are still days Lisa wishes Dan were here, but she has learned to stake her life on the promises and hope of God's Word—a hope not just for eternity but for this earth. For us. Right here, right now.

Out of the tidal wave of a heart attack, out of the grief, out of the suffering, God's faithfulness and mercy remain.

You may not have lost a spouse, but maybe you've lost someone or something you deeply care about. In your grief, you wonder if God is really good—if He can be trusted fully. Don't settle for just getting by or surviving the grief. Reach out to others in prayer and reach out to God. He is near to the brokenhearted.

Faith at the Brink of Death: Michele Cushatt

The phone call came at 8:30 on the Tuesday morning before Thanksgiving Day.

"Michele, it's not good," the doctor said.

Six days before, after doing a biopsy, Michele Cushatt's doctor had assured her there was nothing to worry about. But now, just a few months after her thirty-ninth birthday, Michele found herself diagnosed with a rare, squamous cell carcinoma of the tongue, typically found in smokers. Only, she wasn't a smoker.

In the blink of an eye, cancer rewrote her life as a worst-case scenario and deeply challenged her faith.

In her first three decades of life, Michele had already endured the trials that come with divorce and becoming a single mom. Yet even though there was good that came from the pain—learning to trade her formulaic faith for a deeper faith in the person of Christ—all she could think was: *Really, God, you're going to throw cancer on me now too?*

But the battle was only just beginning. Over the next five years Michele would be diagnosed with tongue cancer two more times, with the cancer coming back more advanced and aggressive each time. To date, she has lost two-thirds of her tongue and has endured excruciating radiation and chemotherapy treatments that took her to the brink of death in order to save her life.

After years of cancer surgeries, treatments, and recovery therapies, Michele has suffered an intense amount of loss and heartache, but she also has gained a faith that circumstances cannot shake. It's not a clean faith; but despite momentary questions, weariness, doubts, and confusion, it is an unshakable one—a faith that believes and hopes, even against all odds.

I was fortunate enough to host Michele on the first episode of my podcast. I'll never forget what she shared as we talked about learning how to thrive in the deep waters of life:

> For years, I wanted to keep my faith small, but God in His great mercy allowed me to go through circumstances that caused my faith to grow to where I always wanted it to be; I just didn't want to go through the hard stuff to get it there. In my suffering, I found myself in a place where I was right next to a Jesus who went through even worse suffering on our behalf. There's something holy and sacred about that. It doesn't take the pain away but gives us a sense of God's divine presence through it all.[5]

In the middle of the raging seas, in the middle of our mess, God is there. He was there for Michele, and He will be there for you too.

Beauty for Ashes: Jamie Clements

After reaching her twenty-second week of pregnancy, Jamie Clements drove with her husband, Justin, to her obstetrician's office, excited for their second ultrasound. By this time, their daughter was about the size of a small spaghetti squash—her lips, eyelids, and eyebrows becoming more distinct with each passing day. They couldn't wait to see her and waited with anticipation as the assistant rubbed cool gel on Jamie's belly while prepping for the sonographer.

Within minutes their daughter appeared on the video monitor, filling Jamie with joy. She was perfect. Absolutely perfect. Or at least she thought she was until the sonographer came in to read the results.

"Jamie, we're concerned about the size of her heart and brain," they said. "We're not entirely sure what this could mean. It could be a sign of Down syndrome or something else. Would you like to abort?"

The question hit Jamie like a punch in the gut. No. Absolutely not. She would never terminate the life of a child God had given her. She resolved to be joyful for whatever God brought their way. And yet as they drove home, she had to admit she wasn't sure if she fully trusted God in the matter. If He gave them a special-needs child, was she ready for that? Honestly, she didn't know.

Sixteen weeks later Jamie went into labor twelve days early, not thinking anything of it. People had babies early all the time. There was nothing abnormal about that. Besides, she was ready to have a natural birth and finally meet her daughter, Remi, face to face.

All birthing plans went out the window, however, when in-between contractions the doctor gave her a twenty-minute notice for an emergency cesarean. In an instant, panic overtook Jamie. What could be wrong? What was happening? None of this made sense. And then everything went black.

Hours later at 1:15 a.m., Jamie opened her eyes to find her entire family surrounding her hospital bed. She still didn't know what was going on, but she had a sinking feeling the situation couldn't be good.

"Where's Remi? Where is my baby?" she asked.

And then the truth came out: Something was terribly wrong with Remi. They didn't know what, but she was in an incubator waiting to be transported to a hospital that could determine the answer. Three agonizing days went by before doctors discovered what was wrong.

"Remi has an incurable infection called toxoplasmosis," they told them. "We're so sorry to tell you this, but she has a one percent chance of survival."

Jamie wanted to believe God for healing, as her entire family and support system were doing. She, along with hundreds of others from her community, prayed for healing. But after thirty-nine days, Remi's life began to slip away. Suddenly, Jamie and Justin had a choice to make. They could put their daughter on life support, or they could trust God and let Him decide the outcome of Remi's life.

With tears welling up in her eyes, Jamie said, "We choose to trust God. His will be done. This little life is not ours to keep."

In what seemed like a hopeless situation, Jamie turned to the Bible for encouragement, which she found in Job 1:21: "The LORD gave and the LORD has taken away; / may the name of the LORD be praised." In the midst of her deepest pain, she knew God had given Remi to her for a reason. Her life was truly a gift, no matter how short it had been; and in the end Jamie knew God would bless her for her faithfulness to Him, just as He had blessed Job. In sharing her story with me, Jamie wrote:

> It has been over five years since I lost Remi, and trust me, I have had many moments where I have questioned God's presence. I have shouted and asked the "Why me?" question that many of us ask when we are suffering. I would have been such a great mom to her and was ready to drop everything to care for her. I had moments where I was bitter and jealous of every other mom on the planet…but I knew I couldn't linger there. Instead, I asked God to help me forward. I asked Him for His love and mercy to rain down on me and consume me. A year and a half later, I had a healthy son, but with prayer over Psalm 37:4, I wanted another girl so badly. God promised me a girl and

delivered her to me on March 7, the day Remi passed away. God's timing is incredible.[6]

God's plans are too wonderful for us to know. Though we can't always understand why God allows suffering, we can trust His love and faithfulness to see us through when we surrender all to Him.

Living in Light of Eternity: Monica Moore

Many of us deal with back pain at one point or another, so when Monica Moore began experiencing some back pain after her forty-eighth birthday, she didn't think anything of it.

I probably lifted too many heavy things, she thought to herself.

But the pain didn't go away like a normal back sprain should. Instead, it grew stronger over time, radiating up and down her spine.

X-rays revealed arthritis, and Monica began receiving regular chiropractic treatments to minimize her symptoms. As the months went on, everything seemed fine until she bent over in one doctor's appointment only to experience excruciating pain.

Concerned, her family physician conducted a few tests, which revealed high protein levels in her blood. This discovery led to more tests with a local oncologist, including an MRI that uncovered the root of Monica's pain: multiple lytic bone lesions all over her body, particularly in her skull, shoulders, back, hips, and femurs.

Monica was diagnosed with stage three multiple myeloma (MM), an incurable form of bone marrow

Though we can't always understand why God allows suffering, we can trust His love and faithfulness to see us through when we surrender all to Him.

plasma cell cancer usually seen in those over the age of sixty. In the presence of her husband and daughter, she shed a few tears; but where anxiety and panic should have taken root, all she felt was peace.

"I feel that knowing the Lord, and who I am in Him, gave me the peace at the time of the diagnosis—and continues to give me peace to this day," Monica told me recently in an email. "I'm not afraid of death. The believer in Jesus never stops living."[7]

After eighteen months of chemotherapy infusions, oral chemotherapies and steroids, bone-strengthening infusions, and an autologous stem-cell transplant, Monica reached complete remission. But her battle is far from over—MM is incurable, and Monica must take a chemo pill to prolong remission as long as she can. This does not come without a host of unpleasant side effects. Because the cancer damaged much of Monica's bones, pain is a constant companion; and the chemo pill makes her prone to developing infections.

As someone who also suffers from chronic unrelenting pain, I know how easy it can be to give in to a bitter, defeated spirit. But Monica? I don't think I've ever seen the woman without a smile on her face. Her joy is undeniable, and she is determined to be a light and a helping hand to everyone she meets.

When I was diagnosed with hEDS, Monica reached out to me to encourage me to keep the faith. (She even sent me an essential oil pain-relief cream that I continue to use to this very day!) When I went back to read our online messaging thread, I was struck once again by her beautiful testimony of what faith can do in a surrendered heart.

> Stay strong! Keep on staying close to the Lord as you have been! He knows what it's like to have suffered on this earth. . . . I find such comfort in that! Also as time goes by, I've gotten more used to my new life and what I can and cannot do and finding joy out of every day, even the days when the tears flow.[8]

Even when the tears flow, there is great hope for those who pursue the Lord and seek to find joy in every moment. That's what faith can do.

Statistics say that Monica has another five years left on this earth. Her response to this?

> I am still a blessed woman and I am not afraid of death. I know that my Savior lives, and I look forward to falling on my knees in front of Him with tears running down my face as I thank Him in person for dying on the cross, saving me from my own sin, and giving me the hope of eternal life in heaven with Him—praising Him with His great, big family.[9]

Monica, I can't wait to be singing right there with you!

This I Know

I don't know what my future holds any more than Heather, Lisa, Michele, Jamie, Monica, or you do. I don't know where God will take my ministry. I don't know how long God will call me to host events or how many more books He'll breathe into my spirit. I don't know how my husband's business will be doing two, let alone seven, years from now. I don't know if I'll receive another major health diagnosis on top of hEDS. I don't know how many kids Alex and I will or will not have due to my health condition. I don't know if God will heal me, or if I'll eventually undergo surgeries for my degenerating joints. I don't know how many bad pain days are ahead. Gracious, I don't even know what I'm going to have for breakfast tomorrow morning (er, wait, actually I do: peanut butter, banana, and dark chocolate oatmeal for life!). But what I do know is this: in the end I hope it's said of me, "Through every high and stormy gale, she kept the faith."

Beloved, I pray you will receive the gift of faith that God so graciously extends for you to claim. And once you do, will you promise me something? Promise me you'll keep it. Today and every day. Not faith in the things of this world but in the person of Christ. And don't just keep it to yourself. Go! Swim! Share it so that others struggling to keep their heads above water in the deep can be saved and strengthened by your testimony and example.

The waves are no match for those who are courageous enough to live by faith.

By the power of the Holy Spirit living within you, you can push back the darkness, doubt, and despair. And I pray that when you do, the only thing you'll choose to drown in is the current of God's love. He is calling you into the deep, into a life of courageous faith.

Keep fighting the good fight of faith, beloved warrior of the deep, and let God overwhelm you with wonder as He helps you overcome. And remember: the waves are no match for those who are courageous enough to live by faith.

GOING DEEPER

1. How do the stories in this chapter inspire you to have unrelenting hope and courageous faith? Is there a particular story that speaks to you, and why?

2. Who are the inspiring warriors of the deep in your own life? What have you learned from them?

3. What will you do to hold tightly to the gift of faith? How can you share it with others who are struggling?

PRAYER

Father, thank You for the Holy Spirit living in me so that I can push back darkness, doubt, and despair. When the waves threaten to take me out or I feel lost at sea, I will not lose faith but will swim even deeper into the current of Your presence and love, trusting that You will give me victory over my circumstances. Thank You for making me a warrior of the deep! In Jesus's name. Amen.

Acknowledgments

Alex: You are the love of my life, and it's a wonder being your wife. Thank you for loving and supporting me so faithfully and unconditionally over the last nine years. I never could have imagined, when we met over frozen shakes, all the adventures God would take us on, including moving to North Carolina while I was writing this book. We've experienced our fair share of ups and downs, but I'm grateful that God has used every single adventure to draw us closer to Him and to each other. There is no one I'd rather swim through this life with than you and Jesus.

Reese: You are more than just my sweet little peanut butter cup. You're an angel in dog form, and you light up my life. Thank you for loving me so well and reminding me to rest as often as I play.

Dad and Mama: Thank you for raising your daughters to live creatively and trust God above all else. Your commitment to love and protect us over the years inspires me, and I hope our children will say the same of Alex and me one day. Thank you for encouraging me to fearlessly and tenaciously pursue the dreams God has placed on my heart. You are two of my biggest cheerleaders, and I'm forever grateful for you.

Ashley: I thank God every day that you're my sister. But more than that, you are also one of my best friends. Thank you for being someone I can always count on and look up to. Your passion and talent for fashion design push me to be the best writer and speaker I can be. PS—It's a KABOOM! flake!

Grandpa and Gramma: Thank you for raising your family to be strong in the faith and to always put Jesus and others first. Your kindness and generosity are astounding, and I love you more than words can say.

Rick and Julie: Thank you for showing us what it looks like to trust God in the midst of overwhelming circumstances. Your marriage is a testament to 1 Corinthians 13:4-8.

Aunt Sharon: Your faith and courage in the face of great pain amaze me. Thank you for always encouraging me to not be afraid of my health issues and to trust God. Our healing is coming, amen? And if not in this life, then when we see Jesus's face.

Heidi, Elli, Evan, and the whole Edman/Gaskill clan: It is a joy and privilege to be a part of your family. Thank you for welcoming me with open hearts and arms—first when Alex and I met in high school and again when we married after college. Our Caribbean trips are some of the greatest memories I have.

Blythe: Thank you for believing in this message and for encouraging me to always practice what I preach. You are more than just an incredible agent to me; you are also a dear friend. Signing with you last year was a huge answer to prayer. God knew what He was doing when He made our paths cross! He is so good.

Sally: I could not have asked for a better editor! God has gifted you with a remarkable talent, and I'm so grateful for both your friendship and expertise.

Heather: To think that God would connect me with a sister in Christ who is a writer and someone with a form of the connective tissue disorder I have—and then move me to the same metro area where you live. His grace abounds, amen? You are one of the most beautiful, courageous, and loving women I've ever known, and it is an immense blessing to do life and ministry with you. I love you, sister.

Barb: You are the first friend I made after stepping into ministry, and oh, what a joy it has been to watch God work in both of our lives over the last four years. Thank you for always being there to pray, brainstorm, and talk about all the things. My life is richer because of you.

Devon, Katie D., and LeeAnn: You have been my friends for the longest, and we've sure made a lot of wonderful memories together. Thank you for encouraging and pushing me all these years and for always believing in me. The three of you will always hold a special place in my heart.

Tracy, Connie, Katie R., Carey, Jami, Christy M., Melinda, Gretchen, Shannon, Lisa, Vanessa, Heather, Katie M., and the whole She Found Joy team: Your love and support have helped carry and sustain me through some pretty rough seas, and I'm so excited about the new things God is doing in and through all of us and She Found Joy. The adventure has only just begun, and I couldn't imagine a better team to have by my side.

Judy: Thank you for believing in me and for championing and encouraging me. I will never forget what you told me last year when I was going through a hard time. "Borrow my hope," you said. Thank you for sharing hope, love, and friendship with me. You're a gift to this world.

Turtle Sisters: Joshua 1:9 forever! Your fellowship is a gift from God and I love y'all so much.

Paul: Thank you for leading the River Valley youth group with passion and authenticity. You left a huge legacy and impacted so many lives, especially mine.

Doc, Kathy, Laura, Chris, and Brad: I'm so grateful for everything you taught me about life and all things writing/English during my time at Concord High School and Ball State University. Your dedication to your students is beautiful, honorable, and life changing. Thank you for helping me become the writer I am today.

To my readers: I am so grateful for the community we share and for the opportunity to journey through the deep waters of life together. Thank you for your support over the years. I am grateful for you!

Jesus: Words cannot possibly describe the awe and gratitude I have for all You are and all You've done for me. Thank You for saving me—not once, not twice, but every time I've fallen. Thank You for never giving up on me and for loving me back to life in You. You are my all in all. You are my everything. I'll see You when You call me home.

Notes

Chapter One

1. Tenth Avenue North, "The Struggle," track 2 on *The Struggle*, Provident Label Group, 2012.

Chapter Two

1. C. S. Lewis, *Till We Have Faces: A Myth Retold* (San Francisco: HarperCollins, 2001), 308.

2. Goo Goo Dolls, "Tattered Edge / You Should Be Happy," track 1 on *You Should Be Happy*, Warner Bros. Records, 2017.

3. "Divided States of America," *Frontline*, January 17-18, 2017, www.pbs.org /wgbh/frontline/film/divided-states-of-america/.

4. Gallup, "Americans' Confidence in Institutions Stays Low," June 13, 2016, http://news.gallup.com/poll/192581/americans-confidence-institutions -stays-low.aspx.

5. Ron Fournier and Sophie Quinton, "How Americans Lost Trust in Our Greatest Institutions," *The Atlantic*, April 20, 2012, www.theatlantic.com/politics /archive/2012/04/how-americans-lost-trust-in-our-greatest-institutions /256.

6. Stephen Bullivant, "Europe's Young Adults and Religion: Findings from the

European Social Survey," St. Mary's University, Twickenham, London, Benedict XVI Centre for Religion and Society, 2018, www.stmarys.ac.uk/research/centres /benedict-xvi/docs/2018-mar-europe-young-people-report-eng.pdf.

7. Pew Research Center, "Religious Landscape Study," 2014, www.pewforum .org/2015/05/12/americas-changing-religious-landscape/.

8. TV Commercial, "The Truth Is Hard," *New York Times*, February 23, 2017, www.youtube.com/watch?v=gY0Fdz350GE.

9. *Merriam-Webster*, s.v. "fail," 2018, www.merriam-webster.com/dictionary /fail.

10. Bryan Walsh, "Ending the War on Fat," *TIME*, June 11, 2014, http://time .com/2863227/ending-the-war-on-fat/.

11. Mark Batterson, *In a Pit with a Lion on a Snowy Day: How to Survive and Thrive When Opportunity Roars* (Colorado Springs: Multnomah, 2016), 49.

Chapter Three

1. National Hurricane Center, "Tropical Cyclone Report: Hurricane Irma," 2017, www.nhc.noaa.gov/data/tcr/AL112017_Irma.pdf.

2. This section of the chapter is adapted from "No Turning Back" by Lauren Gaskill, in *Let Your Light Shine: Being a Light in a Dark World* (North Charleston, SC: Sweet To The Soul Ministries, 2016), 51–52.

3. Auli'i Cravalho, vocalist, "How Far I'll Go," by Lin-Manuel Miranda, track 4 on disc 1 of *Moana* (Original Motion Picture Soundtrack), Walt Disney, 2016.

4. Citipointe Live, "Into the Deep," track 1 on *Into the Deep (Live)*, Citipointe Music, 2016.

Chapter Four

1. Beth Moore, *Praying God's Word: Breaking Free from Spiritual Strongholds* (Nashville: B&H, 2009), 44.

2. Julia Gavaghan, "On This Day: Public Road Speed Record of 268.9 mph Set by Rudolph Caracciola on German Autobahn," *Yahoo News*, January 29, 2014, https://uk.news.yahoo.com/on-this-day--public-road-speed-record-of-268 -9mph-set-by-rudolf-caracciola-on-german-autobahn-122630051.html.

Chapter Five

1. Bible Study Tools, s.v. "pistis," www.biblestudytools.com/lexicons/greek /nas/pistis.html.

2. Bible Study Tools, s.v. "peithô," www.biblestudytools.com/lexicons/greek /nas/peitho.html.

3. *Oxford English Dictionary*, s.v. "practice," 2018, https://en.oxforddictionaries .com/definition/us/practice.

Chapter Six

1. A. W. Tozer, *The Pursuit of God* (Abbotsford, WI: Aneko, 2017), 87.

2. William B. Brahms, *Last Words of Notable People: Final Words of More than 3500 Noteworthy People Throughout History* (Haddonfield, NJ: Reference Desk Press, 2010).

3. Tozer, *Pursuit of God*, 50.

4. Beth Moore, *Breaking Free* (Nashville: LifeWay, 2015), 65.

Chapter Seven

1. Alec Rutherford, *New York Times* interview with Trudy Ederle (August 8, 1926), quoted in Gavin Mortimer, *The Great Swim* (New York: Walker, 2009), 160.

2. Mortimer, *Great Swim*, 186.

3. Mary Ann ———, personal email to author.

4. Priscilla Shirer, *The Armor of God* (Nashville: LifeWay, 2016), 69.

Chapter Eight

1. Rick Warren, *The Purpose Driven Life: What on Earth Am I Here For?* (Grand Rapids, MI: Zondervan, 2002), 29.

2. Jonathan Martin, *How to Survive a Shipwreck* (Grand Rapids: Zondervan, 2016), 115.

Chapter Nine

1. Suzanne Eller, *Come with Me: Discovering the Beauty of Following Where He Leads* (Bloomington, MN: Bethany, 2016), 39.

2. Lauren Gaskill, "How I Got My Prayer Mojo Back," December 1, 2016, http://tsuzanneeller.com/2016/12/01/believing-again/.

3. "President Obama Visited Elkhart, Indiana," YouTube, www.youtube.com/watch?v=1jGWcuPhCYo.

4. Scott Krippayne and Tony Wood, "Even If," track 4 on Kutless, *Believer* (Deluxe Edition), Capitol Christian Music, 2012.

5. Jon Bloom, *Not by Sight* (Wheaton, IL: Crossway, 2013), 83.

6. Barb Roose, conversation with the author.

Chapter Ten

1. Meghan Trainor and Kevin Kadish, "All About That Bass," track 2 on *Title* (Deluxe Edition), Epic Records, 2015.

Chapter Eleven

1. Billy Graham, *Hope for Each Day: Words of Wisdom and Faith* (Nashville: Thomas Nelson, 2017), 12.

2. Beth Moore, *Breaking Free* (Nashville: LifeWay, 2015), 38.

Chapter Twelve

1. Philip Yancey, *Where Is God When It Hurts?* (Grand Rapids: Zondervan, 1990), 251.

2. "Fishermen: We Never Gave Up Hope to Be Saved," NBC News, August 18, 2006, www.nbcnews.com/id/14410580/ns/world_news-americas/t/fishermen-we-never-gave-hope-be-saved/#.WuYxMtPwbOQ.

3. Heather Dixon, "Ready for Hope," in *Journey: A Woman's Guide to Intimacy with God* (Nashville: LifeWay, January 2018).

4. Lisa Appelo, "Life Shattered," June 5, 2014, https://lisaappelo.com/life-shattered/.

5. Michele Cushatt, "Finding Joy in an Undone Life," *She Found Joy* podcast, episode 1, www.laurengaskillinspires.com/finding-joy-when-life-falls-apart/.

6. Jamie Clements, personal interview with the author, February 14, 2018.

7. Monica Moore, email to the author.

8. Monica Moore, online messaging thread with the author.

9. Monica Moore, personal interview with the author, February 13, 2018.